C-3832

THIS IS YOUR **PASSBOOK**® FOR ...

ASSISTANT SIGNALMAN

NLC®

NATIONAL LEARNING CORPORATION®

passbooks.com

PASSBOOK® SERIES

THE *PASSBOOK® SERIES* has been created to prepare applicants and candidates for the ultimate academic battlefield – the examination room.

At some time in our lives, each and every one of us may be required to take an examination – for validation, matriculation, admission, qualification, registration, certification, or licensure.

Based on the assumption that every applicant or candidate has met the basic formal educational standards, has taken the required number of courses, and read the necessary texts, the *PASSBOOK® SERIES* furnishes the one special preparation which may assure passing with confidence, instead of failing with insecurity. Examination questions – together with answers – are furnished as the basic vehicle for study so that the mysteries of the examination and its compounding difficulties may be eliminated or diminished by a sure method.

This book is meant to help you pass your examination provided that you qualify and are serious in your objective.

The entire field is reviewed through the huge store of content information which is succinctly presented through a provocative and challenging approach – the question-and-answer method.

A climate of success is established by furnishing the correct answers at the end of each test.

You soon learn to recognize types of questions, forms of questions, and patterns of questioning. You may even begin to anticipate expected outcomes.

You perceive that many questions are repeated or adapted so that you can gain acute insights, which may enable you to score many sure points.

You learn how to confront new questions, or types of questions, and to attack them confidently and work out the correct answers.

You note objectives and emphases, and recognize pitfalls and dangers, so that you may make positive educational adjustments.

Moreover, you are kept fully informed in relation to new concepts, methods, practices, and directions in the field.

You discover that you arre actually taking the examination all the time: you are preparing for the examination by "taking" an examination, not by reading extraneous and/or supererogatory textbooks.

In short, this PASSBOOK®, used directedly, should be an important factor in helping you to pass your test.

ASSISTANT SIGNALMAN

Assistant Signalman-Communications: Communications work includes but not limited to the installation and maintenance of: pole lines, underground cable systems, tunnel cable systems, wayside and office voice/data/video communications and cable systems, voice/data/video transport systems, electronics and enclosures/huts/rooms, radio systems, security systems, alarm systems. The individual will be responsible to demonstrate sufficient aptitude to learn this information and accept training. The individual must perform all assigned tasks safely and responsibly. The Company provides a training program consisting of both classroom and field training. Failure to qualify as a Signalman within the four (4) training program will result in termination of employment. Qualification as a Signalman requires at a minimum to successfully pass a pole line construction/maintenance test and obtaining of a CDL class "B" license. ***This position requires the climbing of wood poles with gaffs/hooks.

Assistant Signalman-Signal: Signal work includes excavation along the right-of-way for installation of signal cables, air lines, and foundations for signal equipment; trims trees, cut brush and paints various signal equipment; assists qualified mechanic in the assembly, installation and testing of same equipment. Employee must be skilled in the use of various hand and/or power tools and comply with all Company safety rules and policies. The Company provides a training program of up to four (4) years, consisting of both classroom and field training. Failure to qualify as a Signalman within the four (4) year training period will result in termination of employment.

Desired candidates should possess an electrical aptitude, coupled with mechanical ability. This position will require employees to work in construction and/or maintenance functions, which will include the installation of signal and communications equipment, the maintenance of these systems, and troubleshooting of malfunctioning equipment. Candidates considered for employment must be capable of working in all environments (i.e. confined spaces; heights; noisy) and under all weather conditions (i.e. snow; rain; ice; heat.) Successful candidates must also be able to perform construction activities, such as digging, usually for extended periods of time.

The selection procedure includes a written entrance exam on electrical theory/Ohm's Law/Series and Parallel Circuit Analysis and a practical examination on electrical and mechanical aptitude. Additionally, candidates must complete a pre-employment electric/electronic computer-based training program.

SUMMARY OF DUTIES

Assistant Signalman are required to do maintenance work, i.e. dig ditches and climb poles (approximately 30 feet), and install cable. They are also required to maintain an acceptable grade level during their technical training, showing sufficient aptitude to learn information and accept training. This position involves a four-year training program of the individual for the purpose of advancement to Mechanic.

Assistant Signalman are expected to work under the direction of other members of the department and learn the work generally recognized as accruing to communications/ signal department employees

SPECIAL REQUIREMENTS

Employee must show progress in completing the various phases of the signalman's training program in order to be able to qualify for a mechanic's position within four (4) years. Failure to display progress will result in termination of employment. Candidates must pass a written exam and panel interview process. Basic electrical background required, either acquired through formal training and/or practical experience. Pole climbing — communication department employees must be able to pass a preliminary pole climbing test (within first six (6) months of employment). A valid state driver's license is required and CDL B Driver's license must be obtained prior to promotion. A high school diploma or equivalent is required — completion of any training programs dealing with electronics is desired. Prior experience pole line and climbing, field work in any of the following areas: radio, security alarms, telephones, computers, public address system, CCTV and general electronic equipment are desirable.

PHYSICAL ACTIVITIES OF POSITION

This position may require employees to have the ability and stamina to climb and work proficiently on poles and serial structures. Must also be able to lift equipment weighing up to 70 pounds. Will be required to assist others in lifting and moving heavier equipment. Must be able to dig trenches, holes, etc.

WORKING CONDITIONS

Employees are required to work under satisfactory and adverse conditions. Employees must wear safety vest, hardhat, and respirators as dictated by company policy. The above job activities may require the following:
Grinding with power tools within a confined area;
Operating dust, grit or fume-producing power tools or machinery;
Operating sand, grit or shot-blasting tools or machinery;
Performing other work involving acids, toxic materials, gases or fumes that may be nauseating or constitute a respiratory hazard;
Use of emergency generators; and
All other conditions or situations deemed necessary by the company.

SCOPE OF THE EXAMINATION

The written test will consist of basic electrical and electronics, including ohms law, circuit theory and other related areas.

HOW TO TAKE A TEST

I. YOU MUST PASS AN EXAMINATION

A. WHAT EVERY CANDIDATE SHOULD KNOW

Examination applicants often ask us for help in preparing for the written test. What can I study in advance? What kinds of questions will be asked? How will the test be given? How will the papers be graded?

As an applicant for a civil service examination, you may be wondering about some of these things. Our purpose here is to suggest effective methods of advance study and to describe civil service examinations.

Your chances for success on this examination can be increased if you know how to prepare. Those "pre-examination jitters" can be reduced if you know what to expect. You can even experience an adventure in good citizenship if you know why civil service exams are given.

B. WHY ARE CIVIL SERVICE EXAMINATIONS GIVEN?

Civil service examinations are important to you in two ways. As a citizen, you want public jobs filled by employees who know how to do their work. As a job seeker, you want a fair chance to compete for that job on an equal footing with other candidates. The best-known means of accomplishing this two-fold goal is the competitive examination.

Exams are widely publicized throughout the nation. They may be administered for jobs in federal, state, city, municipal, town or village governments or agencies.

Any citizen may apply, with some limitations, such as the age or residence of applicants. Your experience and education may be reviewed to see whether you meet the requirements for the particular examination. When these requirements exist, they are reasonable and applied consistently to all applicants. Thus, a competitive examination may cause you some uneasiness now, but it is your privilege and safeguard.

C. HOW ARE CIVIL SERVICE EXAMS DEVELOPED?

Examinations are carefully written by trained technicians who are specialists in the field known as "psychological measurement," in consultation with recognized authorities in the field of work that the test will cover. These experts recommend the subject matter areas or skills to be tested; only those knowledges or skills important to your success on the job are included. The most reliable books and source materials available are used as references. Together, the experts and technicians judge the difficulty level of the questions.

Test technicians know how to phrase questions so that the problem is clearly stated. Their ethics do not permit "trick" or "catch" questions. Questions may have been tried out on sample groups, or subjected to statistical analysis, to determine their usefulness.

Written tests are often used in combination with performance tests, ratings of training and experience, and oral interviews. All of these measures combine to form the best-known means of finding the right person for the right job.

II. HOW TO PASS THE WRITTEN TEST

A. *NATURE OF THE EXAMINATION*

To prepare intelligently for civil service examinations, you should know how they differ from school examinations you have taken. In school you were assigned certain definite pages to read or subjects to cover. The examination questions were quite detailed and usually emphasized memory. Civil service exams, on the other hand, try to discover your present ability to perform the duties of a position, plus your potentiality to learn these duties. In other words, a civil service exam attempts to predict how successful you will be. Questions cover such a broad area that they cannot be as minute and detailed as school exam questions.

In the public service similar kinds of work, or positions, are grouped together in one "class." This process is known as *position-classification*. All the positions in a class are paid according to the salary range for that class. One class title covers all of these positions, and they are all tested by the same examination.

B. *FOUR BASIC STEPS*

1) **Study the announcement**

How, then, can you know what subjects to study? Our best answer is: "Learn as much as possible about the class of positions for which you've applied." The exam will test the knowledge, skills and abilities needed to do the work.

Your most valuable source of information about the position you want is the official exam announcement. This announcement lists the training and experience qualifications. Check these standards and apply only if you come reasonably close to meeting them.

The brief description of the position in the examination announcement offers some clues to the subjects which will be tested. Think about the job itself. Review the duties in your mind. Can you perform them, or are there some in which you are rusty? Fill in the blank spots in your preparation.

Many jurisdictions preview the written test in the exam announcement by including a section called "Knowledge and Abilities Required," "Scope of the Examination," or some similar heading. Here you will find out specifically what fields will be tested.

2) **Review your own background**

Once you learn in general what the position is all about, and what you need to know to do the work, ask yourself which subjects you already know fairly well and which need improvement. You may wonder whether to concentrate on improving your strong areas or on building some background in your fields of weakness. When the announcement has specified "some knowledge" or "considerable knowledge," or has used adjectives like "beginning principles of..." or "advanced ... methods," you can get a clue as to the number and difficulty of questions to be asked in any given field. More questions, and hence broader coverage, would be included for those subjects which are more important in the work. Now weigh your strengths and weaknesses against the job requirements and prepare accordingly.

3) Determine the level of the position

Another way to tell how intensively you should prepare is to understand the level of the job for which you are applying. Is it the entering level? In other words, is this the position in which beginners in a field of work are hired? Or is it an intermediate or advanced level? Sometimes this is indicated by such words as "Junior" or "Senior" in the class title. Other jurisdictions use Roman numerals to designate the level – Clerk I, Clerk II, for example. The word "Supervisor" sometimes appears in the title. If the level is not indicated by the title, check the description of duties. Will you be working under very close supervision, or will you have responsibility for independent decisions in this work?

4) Choose appropriate study materials

Now that you know the subjects to be examined and the relative amount of each subject to be covered, you can choose suitable study materials. For beginning level jobs, or even advanced ones, if you have a pronounced weakness in some aspect of your training, read a modern, standard textbook in that field. Be sure it is up to date and has general coverage. Such books are normally available at your library, and the librarian will be glad to help you locate one. For entry-level positions, questions of appropriate difficulty are chosen – neither highly advanced questions, nor those too simple. Such questions require careful thought but not advanced training.

If the position for which you are applying is technical or advanced, you will read more advanced, specialized material. If you are already familiar with the basic principles of your field, elementary textbooks would waste your time. Concentrate on advanced textbooks and technical periodicals. Think through the concepts and review difficult problems in your field.

These are all general sources. You can get more ideas on your own initiative, following these leads. For example, training manuals and publications of the government agency which employs workers in your field can be useful, particularly for technical and professional positions. A letter or visit to the government department involved may result in more specific study suggestions, and certainly will provide you with a more definite idea of the exact nature of the position you are seeking.

III. KINDS OF TESTS

Tests are used for purposes other than measuring knowledge and ability to perform specified duties. For some positions, it is equally important to test ability to make adjustments to new situations or to profit from training. In others, basic mental abilities not dependent on information are essential. Questions which test these things may not appear as pertinent to the duties of the position as those which test for knowledge and information. Yet they are often highly important parts of a fair examination. For very general questions, it is almost impossible to help you direct your study efforts. What we can do is to point out some of the more common of these general abilities needed in public service positions and describe some typical questions.

1) General information

Broad, general information has been found useful for predicting job success in some kinds of work. This is tested in a variety of ways, from vocabulary lists to questions about current events. Basic background in some field of work, such as sociology or economics, may be sampled in a group of questions. Often these are principles which have become familiar to most persons through exposure rather than through formal training. It is difficult to advise you how to study for these questions; being alert to the world around you is our best suggestion.

2) Verbal ability

An example of an ability needed in many positions is verbal or language ability. Verbal ability is, in brief, the ability to use and understand words. Vocabulary and grammar tests are typical measures of this ability. Reading comprehension or paragraph interpretation questions are common in many kinds of civil service tests. You are given a paragraph of written material and asked to find its central meaning.

3) Numerical ability

Number skills can be tested by the familiar arithmetic problem, by checking paired lists of numbers to see which are alike and which are different, or by interpreting charts and graphs. In the latter test, a graph may be printed in the test booklet which you are asked to use as the basis for answering questions.

4) Observation

A popular test for law-enforcement positions is the observation test. A picture is shown to you for several minutes, then taken away. Questions about the picture test your ability to observe both details and larger elements.

5) Following directions

In many positions in the public service, the employee must be able to carry out written instructions dependably and accurately. You may be given a chart with several columns, each column listing a variety of information. The questions require you to carry out directions involving the information given in the chart.

6) Skills and aptitudes

Performance tests effectively measure some manual skills and aptitudes. When the skill is one in which you are trained, such as typing or shorthand, you can practice. These tests are often very much like those given in business school or high school courses. For many of the other skills and aptitudes, however, no short-time preparation can be made. Skills and abilities natural to you or that you have developed throughout your lifetime are being tested.

Many of the general questions just described provide all the data needed to answer the questions and ask you to use your reasoning ability to find the answers. Your best preparation for these tests, as well as for tests of facts and ideas, is to be at your physical and mental best. You, no doubt, have your own methods of getting into an exam-taking mood and keeping "in shape." The next section lists some ideas on this subject.

IV. KINDS OF QUESTIONS

Only rarely is the "essay" question, which you answer in narrative form, used in civil service tests. Civil service tests are usually of the short-answer type. Full instructions for answering these questions will be given to you at the examination. But in case this is your first experience with short-answer questions and separate answer sheets, here is what you need to know:

1) Multiple-choice Questions

Most popular of the short-answer questions is the "multiple choice" or "best answer" question. It can be used, for example, to test for factual knowledge, ability to solve problems or judgment in meeting situations found at work.

A multiple-choice question is normally one of three types—

- It can begin with an incomplete statement followed by several possible endings. You are to find the one ending which *best* completes the statement, although some of the others may not be entirely wrong.
- It can also be a complete statement in the form of a question which is answered by choosing one of the statements listed.
- It can be in the form of a problem – again you select the best answer.

Here is an example of a multiple-choice question with a discussion which should give you some clues as to the method for choosing the right answer:

When an employee has a complaint about his assignment, the action which will *best* help him overcome his difficulty is to
   A. discuss his difficulty with his coworkers
   B. take the problem to the head of the organization
   C. take the problem to the person who gave him the assignment
   D. say nothing to anyone about his complaint

In answering this question, you should study each of the choices to find which is best. Consider choice "A" – Certainly an employee may discuss his complaint with fellow employees, but no change or improvement can result, and the complaint remains unresolved. Choice "B" is a poor choice since the head of the organization probably does not know what assignment you have been given, and taking your problem to him is known as "going over the head" of the supervisor. The supervisor, or person who made the assignment, is the person who can clarify it or correct any injustice. Choice "C" is, therefore, correct. To say nothing, as in choice "D," is unwise. Supervisors have and interest in knowing the problems employees are facing, and the employee is seeking a solution to his problem.

2) True/False Questions

The "true/false" or "right/wrong" form of question is sometimes used. Here a complete statement is given. Your job is to decide whether the statement is right or wrong.

SAMPLE: A roaming cell-phone call to a nearby city costs less than a non-roaming call to a distant city.

This statement is wrong, or false, since roaming calls are more expensive.
This is not a complete list of all possible question forms, although most of the others are variations of these common types. You will always get complete directions for

answering questions. Be sure you understand *how* to mark your answers – ask questions until you do.

V. RECORDING YOUR ANSWERS

Computer terminals are used more and more today for many different kinds of exams.

For an examination with very few applicants, you may be told to record your answers in the test booklet itself. Separate answer sheets are much more common. If this separate answer sheet is to be scored by machine – and this is often the case – it is highly important that you mark your answers correctly in order to get credit.

An electronic scoring machine is often used in civil service offices because of the speed with which papers can be scored. Machine-scored answer sheets must be marked with a pencil, which will be given to you. This pencil has a high graphite content which responds to the electronic scoring machine. As a matter of fact, stray dots may register as answers, so do not let your pencil rest on the answer sheet while you are pondering the correct answer. Also, if your pencil lead breaks or is otherwise defective, ask for another.

Since the answer sheet will be dropped in a slot in the scoring machine, be careful not to bend the corners or get the paper crumpled.

The answer sheet normally has five vertical columns of numbers, with 30 numbers to a column. These numbers correspond to the question numbers in your test booklet. After each number, going across the page are four or five pairs of dotted lines. These short dotted lines have small letters or numbers above them. The first two pairs may also have a "T" or "F" above the letters. This indicates that the first two pairs only are to be used if the questions are of the true-false type. If the questions are multiple choice, disregard the "T" and "F" and pay attention only to the small letters or numbers.

Answer your questions in the manner of the sample that follows:

32. The largest city in the United States is
   A. Washington, D.C.
   B. New York City
   C. Chicago
   D. Detroit
   E. San Francisco

1) Choose the answer you think is best. (New York City is the largest, so "B" is correct.)
2) Find the row of dotted lines numbered the same as the question you are answering. (Find row number 32)
3) Find the pair of dotted lines corresponding to the answer. (Find the pair of lines under the mark "B.")
4) Make a solid black mark between the dotted lines.

VI. BEFORE THE TEST

Common sense will help you find procedures to follow to get ready for an examination. Too many of us, however, overlook these sensible measures. Indeed, nervousness and fatigue have been found to be the most serious reasons why applicants fail to do their best on civil service tests. Here is a list of reminders:

- Begin your preparation early – Don't wait until the last minute to go scurrying around for books and materials or to find out what the position is all about.
- Prepare continuously – An hour a night for a week is better than an all-night cram session. This has been definitely established. What is more, a night a week for a month will return better dividends than crowding your study into a shorter period of time.
- Locate the place of the exam – You have been sent a notice telling you when and where to report for the examination. If the location is in a different town or otherwise unfamiliar to you, it would be well to inquire the best route and learn something about the building.
- Relax the night before the test – Allow your mind to rest. Do not study at all that night. Plan some mild recreation or diversion; then go to bed early and get a good night's sleep.
- Get up early enough to make a leisurely trip to the place for the test – This way unforeseen events, traffic snarls, unfamiliar buildings, etc. will not upset you.
- Dress comfortably – A written test is not a fashion show. You will be known by number and not by name, so wear something comfortable.
- Leave excess paraphernalia at home – Shopping bags and odd bundles will get in your way. You need bring only the items mentioned in the official notice you received; usually everything you need is provided. Do not bring reference books to the exam. They will only confuse those last minutes and be taken away from you when in the test room.
- Arrive somewhat ahead of time – If because of transportation schedules you must get there very early, bring a newspaper or magazine to take your mind off yourself while waiting.
- Locate the examination room – When you have found the proper room, you will be directed to the seat or part of the room where you will sit. Sometimes you are given a sheet of instructions to read while you are waiting. Do not fill out any forms until you are told to do so; just read them and be prepared.
- Relax and prepare to listen to the instructions
- If you have any physical problem that may keep you from doing your best, be sure to tell the test administrator. If you are sick or in poor health, you really cannot do your best on the exam. You can come back and take the test some other time.

VII. AT THE TEST

The day of the test is here and you have the test booklet in your hand. The temptation to get going is very strong. Caution! There is more to success than knowing the right answers. You must know how to identify your papers and understand variations in the type of short-answer question used in this particular examination. Follow these suggestions for maximum results from your efforts:

1) Cooperate with the monitor

The test administrator has a duty to create a situation in which you can be as much at ease as possible. He will give instructions, tell you when to begin, check to see that you are marking your answer sheet correctly, and so on. He is not there to guard you, although he will see that your competitors do not take unfair advantage. He wants to help you do your best.

2) Listen to all instructions

Don't jump the gun! Wait until you understand all directions. In most civil service tests you get more time than you need to answer the questions. So don't be in a hurry. Read each word of instructions until you clearly understand the meaning. Study the examples, listen to all announcements and follow directions. Ask questions if you do not understand what to do.

3) Identify your papers

Civil service exams are usually identified by number only. You will be assigned a number; you must not put your name on your test papers. Be sure to copy your number correctly. Since more than one exam may be given, copy your exact examination title.

4) Plan your time

Unless you are told that a test is a "speed" or "rate of work" test, speed itself is usually not important. Time enough to answer all the questions will be provided, but this does not mean that you have all day. An overall time limit has been set. Divide the total time (in minutes) by the number of questions to determine the approximate time you have for each question.

5) Do not linger over difficult questions

If you come across a difficult question, mark it with a paper clip (useful to have along) and come back to it when you have been through the booklet. One caution if you do this – be sure to skip a number on your answer sheet as well. Check often to be sure that you have not lost your place and that you are marking in the row numbered the same as the question you are answering.

6) Read the questions

Be sure you know what the question asks! Many capable people are unsuccessful because they failed to *read* the questions correctly.

7) Answer all questions

Unless you have been instructed that a penalty will be deducted for incorrect answers, it is better to guess than to omit a question.

8) Speed tests

It is often better NOT to guess on speed tests. It has been found that on timed tests people are tempted to spend the last few seconds before time is called in marking answers at random – without even reading them – in the hope of picking up a few extra points. To discourage this practice, the instructions may warn you that your score will be "corrected" for guessing. That is, a penalty will be applied. The incorrect answers will be deducted from the correct ones, or some other penalty formula will be used.

9) Review your answers

   If you finish before time is called, go back to the questions you guessed or omitted to give them further thought. Review other answers if you have time.

10) Return your test materials

   If you are ready to leave before others have finished or time is called, take ALL your materials to the monitor and leave quietly. Never take any test material with you. The monitor can discover whose papers are not complete, and taking a test booklet may be grounds for disqualification.

VIII. EXAMINATION TECHNIQUES

1) Read the general instructions carefully. These are usually printed on the first page of the exam booklet. As a rule, these instructions refer to the timing of the examination; the fact that you should not start work until the signal and must stop work at a signal, etc. If there are any *special* instructions, such as a choice of questions to be answered, make sure that you note this instruction carefully.

2) When you are ready to start work on the examination, that is as soon as the signal has been given, read the instructions to each question booklet, underline any key words or phrases, such as *least, best, outline, describe* and the like. In this way you will tend to answer as requested rather than discover on reviewing your paper that you *listed without describing*, that you selected the *worst* choice rather than the *best* choice, etc.

3) If the examination is of the objective or multiple-choice type – that is, each question will also give a series of possible answers: A, B, C or D, and you are called upon to select the best answer and write the letter next to that answer on your answer paper – it is advisable to start answering each question in turn. There may be anywhere from 50 to 100 such questions in the three or four hours allotted and you can see how much time would be taken if you read through all the questions before beginning to answer any. Furthermore, if you come across a question or group of questions which you know would be difficult to answer, it would undoubtedly affect your handling of all the other questions.

4) If the examination is of the essay type and contains but a few questions, it is a moot point as to whether you should read all the questions before starting to answer any one. Of course, if you are given a choice – say five out of seven and the like – then it is essential to read all the questions so you can eliminate the two that are most difficult. If, however, you are asked to answer all the questions, there may be danger in trying to answer the easiest one first because you may find that you will spend too much time on it. The best technique is to answer the first question, then proceed to the second, etc.

5) Time your answers. Before the exam begins, write down the time it started, then add the time allowed for the examination and write down the time it must be completed, then divide the time available somewhat as follows:

- If 3-1/2 hours are allowed, that would be 210 minutes. If you have 80 objective-type questions, that would be an average of 2-1/2 minutes per question. Allow yourself no more than 2 minutes per question, or a total of 160 minutes, which will permit about 50 minutes to review.
- If for the time allotment of 210 minutes there are 7 essay questions to answer, that would average about 30 minutes a question. Give yourself only 25 minutes per question so that you have about 35 minutes to review.

6) The most important instruction is to *read each question* and make sure you know what is wanted. The second most important instruction is to *time yourself properly* so that you answer every question. The third most important instruction is to *answer every question*. Guess if you have to but include something for each question. Remember that you will receive no credit for a blank and will probably receive some credit if you write something in answer to an essay question. If you guess a letter – say "B" for a multiple-choice question – you may have guessed right. If you leave a blank as an answer to a multiple-choice question, the examiners may respect your feelings but it will not add a point to your score. Some exams may penalize you for wrong answers, so in such cases *only*, you may not want to guess unless you have some basis for your answer.

7) Suggestions
   a. Objective-type questions
      1. Examine the question booklet for proper sequence of pages and questions
      2. Read all instructions carefully
      3. Skip any question which seems too difficult; return to it after all other questions have been answered
      4. Apportion your time properly; do not spend too much time on any single question or group of questions
      5. Note and underline key words – *all, most, fewest, least, best, worst, same, opposite,* etc.
      6. Pay particular attention to negatives
      7. Note unusual option, e.g., unduly long, short, complex, different or similar in content to the body of the question
      8. Observe the use of "hedging" words – *probably, may, most likely,* etc.
      9. Make sure that your answer is put next to the same number as the question
      10. Do not second-guess unless you have good reason to believe the second answer is definitely more correct
      11. Cross out original answer if you decide another answer is more accurate; do not erase until you are ready to hand your paper in
      12. Answer all questions; guess unless instructed otherwise
      13. Leave time for review

   b. Essay questions
      1. Read each question carefully
      2. Determine exactly what is wanted. Underline key words or phrases.
      3. Decide on outline or paragraph answer

4. Include many different points and elements unless asked to develop any one or two points or elements
5. Show impartiality by giving pros and cons unless directed to select one side only
6. Make and write down any assumptions you find necessary to answer the questions
7. Watch your English, grammar, punctuation and choice of words
8. Time your answers; don't crowd material

8) Answering the essay question

Most essay questions can be answered by framing the specific response around several key words or ideas. Here are a few such key words or ideas:

M's: manpower, materials, methods, money, management
P's: purpose, program, policy, plan, procedure, practice, problems, pitfalls, personnel, public relations
  a. Six basic steps in handling problems:
    1. Preliminary plan and background development
    2. Collect information, data and facts
    3. Analyze and interpret information, data and facts
    4. Analyze and develop solutions as well as make recommendations
    5. Prepare report and sell recommendations
    6. Install recommendations and follow up effectiveness

  b. Pitfalls to avoid
    1. *Taking things for granted* – A statement of the situation does not necessarily imply that each of the elements is necessarily true; for example, a complaint may be invalid and biased so that all that can be taken for granted is that a complaint has been registered
    2. *Considering only one side of a situation* – Wherever possible, indicate several alternatives and then point out the reasons you selected the best one
    3. *Failing to indicate follow up* – Whenever your answer indicates action on your part, make certain that you will take proper follow-up action to see how successful your recommendations, procedures or actions turn out to be
    4. *Taking too long in answering any single question* – Remember to time your answers properly

IX. AFTER THE TEST

Scoring procedures differ in detail among civil service jurisdictions although the general principles are the same. Whether the papers are hand-scored or graded by machine we have described, they are nearly always graded by number. That is, the person who marks the paper knows only the number – never the name – of the applicant. Not until all the papers have been graded will they be matched with names. If other tests, such as training and experience or oral interview ratings have been given, scores will be combined. Different parts of the examination usually have different weights. For example, the written test might count 60 percent of the final grade, and a rating of training and experience 40 percent. In many jurisdictions, veterans will have a certain number of points added to their grades.

After the final grade has been determined, the names are placed in grade order and an eligible list is established. There are various methods for resolving ties between those who get the same final grade – probably the most common is to place first the name of the person whose application was received first. Job offers are made from the eligible list in the order the names appear on it. You will be notified of your grade and your rank as soon as all these computations have been made. This will be done as rapidly as possible.

People who are found to meet the requirements in the announcement are called "eligibles." Their names are put on a list of eligible candidates. An eligible's chances of getting a job depend on how high he stands on this list and how fast agencies are filling jobs from the list.

When a job is to be filled from a list of eligibles, the agency asks for the names of people on the list of eligibles for that job. When the civil service commission receives this request, it sends to the agency the names of the three people highest on this list. Or, if the job to be filled has specialized requirements, the office sends the agency the names of the top three persons who meet these requirements from the general list.

The appointing officer makes a choice from among the three people whose names were sent to him. If the selected person accepts the appointment, the names of the others are put back on the list to be considered for future openings.

That is the rule in hiring from all kinds of eligible lists, whether they are for typist, carpenter, chemist, or something else. For every vacancy, the appointing officer has his choice of any one of the top three eligibles on the list. This explains why the person whose name is on top of the list sometimes does not get an appointment when some of the persons lower on the list do. If the appointing officer chooses the second or third eligible, the No. 1 eligible does not get a job at once, but stays on the list until he is appointed or the list is terminated.

X. HOW TO PASS THE INTERVIEW TEST

The examination for which you applied requires an oral interview test. You have already taken the written test and you are now being called for the interview test – the final part of the formal examination.

You may think that it is not possible to prepare for an interview test and that there are no procedures to follow during an interview. Our purpose is to point out some things you can do in advance that will help you and some good rules to follow and pitfalls to avoid while you are being interviewed.

What is an interview supposed to test?

The written examination is designed to test the technical knowledge and competence of the candidate; the oral is designed to evaluate intangible qualities, not readily measured otherwise, and to establish a list showing the relative fitness of each candidate – as measured against his competitors – for the position sought. Scoring is not on the basis of "right" and "wrong," but on a sliding scale of values ranging from "not passable" to "outstanding." As a matter of fact, it is possible to achieve a relatively low score without a single "incorrect" answer because of evident weakness in the qualities being measured.

Occasionally, an examination may consist entirely of an oral test – either an individual or a group oral. In such cases, information is sought concerning the technical knowledges and abilities of the candidate, since there has been no written examination for this purpose. More commonly, however, an oral test is used to supplement a written examination.

Who conducts interviews?

The composition of oral boards varies among different jurisdictions. In nearly all, a representative of the personnel department serves as chairman. One of the members of the board may be a representative of the department in which the candidate would work. In some cases, "outside experts" are used, and, frequently, a businessman or some other representative of the general public is asked to serve. Labor and management or other special groups may be represented. The aim is to secure the services of experts in the appropriate field.

However the board is composed, it is a good idea (and not at all improper or unethical) to ascertain in advance of the interview who the members are and what groups they represent. When you are introduced to them, you will have some idea of their backgrounds and interests, and at least you will not stutter and stammer over their names.

What should be done before the interview?

While knowledge about the board members is useful and takes some of the surprise element out of the interview, there is other preparation which is more substantive. It *is* possible to prepare for an oral interview – in several ways:

1) Keep a copy of your application and review it carefully before the interview

This may be the only document before the oral board, and the starting point of the interview. Know what education and experience you have listed there, and the sequence and dates of all of it. Sometimes the board will ask you to review the highlights of your experience for them; you should not have to hem and haw doing it.

2) Study the class specification and the examination announcement

Usually, the oral board has one or both of these to guide them. The qualities, characteristics or knowledges required by the position sought are stated in these documents. They offer valuable clues as to the nature of the oral interview. For example, if the job involves supervisory responsibilities, the announcement will usually indicate that knowledge of modern supervisory methods and the qualifications of the candidate as a supervisor will be tested. If so, you can expect such questions, frequently in the form of a hypothetical situation which you are expected to solve. NEVER go into an oral without knowledge of the duties and responsibilities of the job you seek.

3) Think through each qualification required

Try to visualize the kind of questions you would ask if you were a board member. How well could you answer them? Try especially to appraise your own knowledge and background in each area, *measured against the job sought*, and identify any areas in which you are weak. Be critical and realistic – do not flatter yourself.

4) Do some general reading in areas in which you feel you may be weak

For example, if the job involves supervision and your past experience has NOT, some general reading in supervisory methods and practices, particularly in the field of human relations, might be useful. Do NOT study agency procedures or detailed manuals. The oral board will be testing your understanding and capacity, not your memory.

5) Get a good night's sleep and watch your general health and mental attitude

You will want a clear head at the interview. Take care of a cold or any other minor ailment, and of course, no hangovers.

What should be done on the day of the interview?

Now comes the day of the interview itself. Give yourself plenty of time to get there. Plan to arrive somewhat ahead of the scheduled time, particularly if your appointment is in the fore part of the day. If a previous candidate fails to appear, the board might be ready for you a bit early. By early afternoon an oral board is almost invariably behind schedule if there are many candidates, and you may have to wait. Take along a book or magazine to read, or your application to review, but leave any extraneous material in the waiting room when you go in for your interview. In any event, relax and compose yourself.

The matter of dress is important. The board is forming impressions about you – from your experience, your manners, your attitude, and your appearance. Give your personal appearance careful attention. Dress your best, but not your flashiest. Choose conservative, appropriate clothing, and be sure it is immaculate. This is a business interview, and your appearance should indicate that you regard it as such. Besides, being well groomed and properly dressed will help boost your confidence.

Sooner or later, someone will call your name and escort you into the interview room. *This is it.* From here on you are on your own. It is too late for any more preparation. But remember, you asked for this opportunity to prove your fitness, and you are here because your request was granted.

What happens when you go in?

The usual sequence of events will be as follows: The clerk (who is often the board stenographer) will introduce you to the chairman of the oral board, who will introduce you to the other members of the board. Acknowledge the introductions before you sit down. Do not be surprised if you find a microphone facing you or a stenotypist sitting by. Oral interviews are usually recorded in the event of an appeal or other review.

Usually the chairman of the board will open the interview by reviewing the highlights of your education and work experience from your application – primarily for the benefit of the other members of the board, as well as to get the material into the record. Do not interrupt or comment unless there is an error or significant misinterpretation; if that is the case, do not hesitate. But do not quibble about insignificant matters. Also, he will usually ask you some question about your education, experience or your present job – partly to get you to start talking and to establish the interviewing "rapport." He may start the actual questioning, or turn it over to one of the other members. Frequently, each member undertakes the questioning on a particular area, one in which he is perhaps most competent, so you can expect each member to participate in the examination. Because time is limited, you may also expect some rather abrupt switches in the direction the questioning takes, so do not be upset by it. Normally, a board member will not pursue a single line of questioning unless he discovers a particular strength or weakness.

After each member has participated, the chairman will usually ask whether any member has any further questions, then will ask you if you have anything you wish to add. Unless you are expecting this question, it may floor you. Worse, it may start you off on an extended, extemporaneous speech. The board is not usually seeking more information. The question is principally to offer you a last opportunity to present further qualifications or to indicate that you have nothing to add. So, if you feel that a significant qualification or characteristic has been overlooked, it is proper to point it out in a sentence or so. Do not compliment the board on the thoroughness of their examination – they have been sketchy, and you know it. If you wish, merely say, "No thank you, I have nothing further to add." This is a point where you can "talk yourself out" of a good impression or fail to present an important bit of information. Remember, *you close the interview yourself.*

The chairman will then say, "That is all, Mr. _____, thank you." Do not be startled; the interview is over, and quicker than you think. Thank him, gather your belongings and take your leave. Save your sigh of relief for the other side of the door.

How to put your best foot forward

Throughout this entire process, you may feel that the board individually and collectively is trying to pierce your defenses, seek out your hidden weaknesses and embarrass and confuse you. Actually, this is not true. They are obliged to make an appraisal of your qualifications for the job you are seeking, and they want to see you in your best light. Remember, they must interview all candidates and a non-cooperative candidate may become a failure in spite of their best efforts to bring out his qualifications. Here are 15 suggestions that will help you:

1) Be natural – Keep your attitude confident, not cocky

If you are not confident that you can do the job, do not expect the board to be. Do not apologize for your weaknesses, try to bring out your strong points. The board is interested in a positive, not negative, presentation. Cockiness will antagonize any board member and make him wonder if you are covering up a weakness by a false show of strength.

2) Get comfortable, but don't lounge or sprawl

Sit erectly but not stiffly. A careless posture may lead the board to conclude that you are careless in other things, or at least that you are not impressed by the importance of the occasion. Either conclusion is natural, even if incorrect. Do not fuss with your clothing, a pencil or an ashtray. Your hands may occasionally be useful to emphasize a point; do not let them become a point of distraction.

3) Do not wisecrack or make small talk

This is a serious situation, and your attitude should show that you consider it as such. Further, the time of the board is limited – they do not want to waste it, and neither should you.

4) Do not exaggerate your experience or abilities

In the first place, from information in the application or other interviews and sources, the board may know more about you than you think. Secondly, you probably will not get away with it. An experienced board is rather adept at spotting such a situation, so do not take the chance.

5) If you know a board member, do not make a point of it, yet do not hide it

Certainly you are not fooling him, and probably not the other members of the board. Do not try to take advantage of your acquaintanceship – it will probably do you little good.

6) Do not dominate the interview

Let the board do that. They will give you the clues – do not assume that you have to do all the talking. Realize that the board has a number of questions to ask you, and do not try to take up all the interview time by showing off your extensive knowledge of the answer to the first one.

7) Be attentive

You only have 20 minutes or so, and you should keep your attention at its sharpest throughout. When a member is addressing a problem or question to you, give him your undivided attention. Address your reply principally to him, but do not exclude the other board members.

8) Do not interrupt

A board member may be stating a problem for you to analyze. He will ask you a question when the time comes. Let him state the problem, and wait for the question.

9) Make sure you understand the question

Do not try to answer until you are sure what the question is. If it is not clear, restate it in your own words or ask the board member to clarify it for you. However, do not haggle about minor elements.

10) Reply promptly but not hastily

A common entry on oral board rating sheets is "candidate responded readily," or "candidate hesitated in replies." Respond as promptly and quickly as you can, but do not jump to a hasty, ill-considered answer.

11) Do not be peremptory in your answers

A brief answer is proper – but do not fire your answer back. That is a losing game from your point of view. The board member can probably ask questions much faster than you can answer them.

12) Do not try to create the answer you think the board member wants

He is interested in what kind of mind you have and how it works – not in playing games. Furthermore, he can usually spot this practice and will actually grade you down on it.

13) Do not switch sides in your reply merely to agree with a board member

Frequently, a member will take a contrary position merely to draw you out and to see if you are willing and able to defend your point of view. Do not start a debate, yet do not surrender a good position. If a position is worth taking, it is worth defending.

14) Do not be afraid to admit an error in judgment if you are shown to be wrong

The board knows that you are forced to reply without any opportunity for careful consideration. Your answer may be demonstrably wrong. If so, admit it and get on with the interview.

15) Do not dwell at length on your present job

The opening question may relate to your present assignment. Answer the question but do not go into an extended discussion. You are being examined for a *new* job, not your present one. As a matter of fact, try to phrase ALL your answers in terms of the job for which you are being examined.

Basis of Rating

Probably you will forget most of these "do's" and "don'ts" when you walk into the oral interview room. Even remembering them all will not ensure you a passing grade. Perhaps you did not have the qualifications in the first place. But remembering them will help you to put your best foot forward, without treading on the toes of the board members.

Rumor and popular opinion to the contrary notwithstanding, an oral board wants you to make the best appearance possible. They know you are under pressure – but they also want to see how you respond to it as a guide to what your reaction would be under the pressures of the job you seek. They will be influenced by the degree of poise you display, the personal traits you show and the manner in which you respond.

ABOUT THIS BOOK

This book contains tests divided into Examination Sections. Go through each test, answering every question in the margin. At the end of each test look at the answer key and check your answers. On the ones you got wrong, look at the right answer choice and learn. Do not fill in the answers first. Do not memorize the questions and answers, but understand the answer and principles involved. On your test, the questions will likely be different from the samples. Questions are changed and new ones added. If you understand these past questions you should have success with any changes that arise. Tests may consist of several types of questions. We have additional books on each subject should more study be advisable or necessary for you. Finally, the more you study, the better prepared you will be. This book is intended to be the last thing you study before you walk into the examination room. Prior study of relevant texts is also recommended. NLC publishes some of these in our Fundamental Series. Knowledge and good sense are important factors in passing your exam. Good luck also helps. So now study this Passbook, absorb the material contained within and take that knowledge into the examination. Then do your best to pass that exam.

———

EXAMINATION SECTION

EXAMINATION SECTION
TEST 1

DIRECTIONS: Each question or incomplete statement is followed by several suggested answers or completions. Select the one that BEST answers the question or completes the statement. *PRINT THE LETTER OF THE CORRECT ANSWER IN THE SPACE AT THE RIGHT.*

1. Which of the following capacitors could be damaged by a reversal in polarity? A(n) _____ capacitor.   1._____

    A. ceramic   B. paper   C. mica
    D. electrolytic   E. vacuum

2. If the current through a resistor is 6 amperes and the voltage drop across it is 100 volts, what is the approximate value of the resistor in ohm(s)?   2._____

    A. 1660   B. 166   C. 16.6   D. 1.66   E. 0.0166

3. What is the CORRECT use for an arbor press?   3._____

    A. Bending sheet metal   B. Driving self-tapping screws
    C. Removing screws   D. Removing "C" rings
    E. Removing bearings from shafts

4. Which one of the following is a tensioning device in bulk-belt-type conveyor systems? _____ take-up.   4._____

    A. Spring   B. Power   C. Hydraulic
    D. Fluid coupled   E. Flexible coupled

5. When $X_L = X_C$ in a series circuit, what condition exists?   5._____

    A. The circuit impedance is increasing
    B. The circuit is at resonant frequency
    C. The circuit current is minimum
    D. The circuit has no e.m.f. at this time
    E. None of the above

6. Which of the following pieces of information is NOT normally found on a schematic diagram?   6._____

    A. Functional stage name   B. Supply voltages
    C. Part symbols   D. Part values
    E. Physical location of parts

7. When a single-phase induction motor drawing 24 amps at 120 VAC is re-connected to 240 VAC, what will be the amperage at 240 VAC? _____ amps.   7._____

    A. 6   B. 8   C. 12   D. 24   E. 36

8. Which one of the following meters measures the SMALLEST current?   8.____

    A. Kilometer   B. Milliammeter   C. Microvoltmeter
    D. Millivoltmeter   E. Kilovoltmeter

9. If the current through a 1000-ohm resistor is 3 milliamperes, the voltage drop   9.____
    across the resistor is _____ volt(s).

    A. 1   B. 2.5   C. 3   D. 30   E. 300

10. The normally closed contacts of a relay are open when its solenoid is energized
    with VDC. The voltage at which the contacts re-close will be

    A. dependent upon the current through the contacts
    B. dependent upon the voltage applied to the contacts
    C. 24 VDC through the coil
    D. more than 24 VDC through the contacts
    E. less than 24 VDC through the coil

11. Electrical energy is converted to mechanical rotation by what component in the
    electric motor?

    A. Armature   B. Commutator   C. Field
    D. Start windings   E. Stator

12. Ohm's Law expresses the basic relationship of

    A. current, voltage, and resistance
    B. current, voltage, and power
    C. current, power, and resistance
    D. resistance, impedance, and voltage
    E. resistance, power, and impedance

13. In parallel circuits, the voltage is *always*

    A. variable   B. constant   C. alternating
    D. fluctuating   E. sporadic

14. Which one of the following is used as a voltage divider?

    A. Rotary converter   B. Potentiometer   C. Relay
    D. Circuit breaker   E. Voltmeter

Question 15.

Question 15 is based on the following diagram.

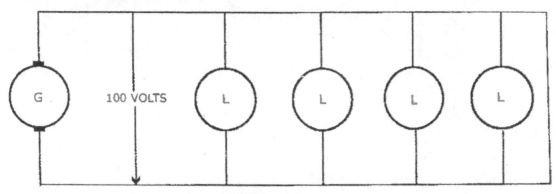

CURRENT IN EACH LAMP 1/2 AMPERE

15. What is the resistance of the entire circuit? _____ ohms.   15.____

    A. 15   B. 25   C. 35   D. 45   E. 50

16. Which one of the following tools is used to bring a bore to a specified   16.____
    tolerance?

    A. Tap   B. Reamer   C. Countersink
    D. Counterbore   E. Center drill

17. The primary function of a take-up pulley in a belt conveyor is to   17.____

    A. carry the belt on the return trip
    B. track the belt
    C. maintain the proper belt tension
    D. change the direction of the belt
    E. regulate the speed of the belt

Question 18.

Question 18 is based on the following diagram.

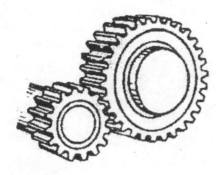

18. What is the name of the gears?   18.____

    A. Spur external   B. Spur internal   C. Helical
    D. Herringbone   D. Worm

Question 19.

Question 19 is based on the following diagram.

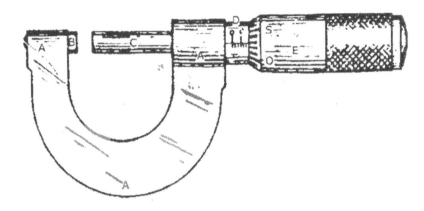

19. The part labeled D is the

19.____

    A. sleeve   B. thimble   C. frame
    D. anvil   E. pindle

Question 20.

Question 20 is based on the following symbol.

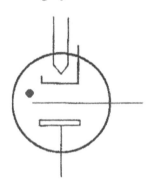

20. This symbol represents a _____ tube.

20.____

    A. thyratron vacuum   B. thyratron gas
    C. variable-mu vacuum   D. variable-mu gas
    E. vacuum photo

21. A diode can be substituted for which one of the following?

21.____

    A. Transformer   B. Relay   C. Rectifier
    D. Condenser   E. Rheostat

Question 22.

Question 22 is based on the following diagram.

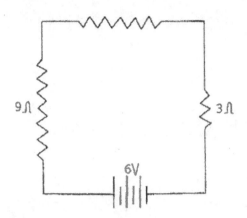

22. The rate of amperes flowing in the circuit is: 22._____

    A. .03 1/3   B. .18   C. .24
    D. .30 1/3   E. .33 1/3

23. The firing point in a thyratron tube is *most usually* controlled by the   23._____

    A. cathode   B. grid   C. plate
    D. heater   E. envelope

Questions 24-25.

Questions 24 and 25 shall be answered in accordance with the diagram below.

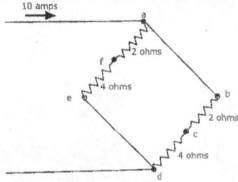

24. With reference to the above diagram, the voltage difference between   24._____
    points c and f is, *most nearly*, in volts,

    A. 40   B. 20   C. 10   D. 5   E. 0

25. With reference to the above diagram, the current flowing through the resistance   25._____
    c d is, *most nearly*, in amperes,

    A. 10   B. 5   C. 4   D. 2   E. 1

KEY (CORRECT ANSWERS)

1.	D	6.	E	11.	A	16.	B	21.	C
2.	C	7.	C	12.	A	17.	C	22.	E
3.	E	8.	B	13.	B	18.	A	23.	B
4.	A	9.	C	14.	B	19.	A	24.	E
5.	B	10.	E	15.	E	20.	B	25.	B

EXAMINATION SECTION
TEST 1

DIRECTIONS: Each question or incomplete statement is followed by several suggested answers or completions. Select the one that BEST answers the question or completes the statement. *PRINT THE LETTER OF THE CORRECT ANSWER IN THE SPACE AT THE RIGHT.*

1. Two gears are meshed. The first gear has 20 teeth per inch and is rotating at 500 rpms. What is the speed of the second gear if it has 40 teeth per inch? _____ rpms.   1._____

    A. 500   B. 400   C. 250   D. 200

2. With two meshed gears, the first gear rotates at 100 rpms, the second gear rotates at 2000 rpms and has 10 teeth per inch.
The first gear has _____ number of teeth per inch.   2._____

    A. 200   B. 100   C. 50   D. 150

3. Two pulleys are connected. The first pulley has a diameter of 5 inches; the second pulley has a diameter of 15 inches and rotates at 25 rpms.
The speed of the first pulley is _____ rpms.   3._____

    A. 30   B. 75   C. 200   D. 400

4. Of two connected pulleys, the first has a radius of 10 inches and rotates at 50 rpms; the second rotates at 25 rpms.
The diameter of the second pulley is _____ inches.   4._____

    A. 40   B. 30   C. 20   D. 10

5. Two pulleys are connected. The first pulley rotates at 75 rpms; the second pulley rotates at 100 rpms and has a diameter of 9 inches.
The diameter of the first pulley is _____ inches.   5._____

    A. 10   B. 12   C. 15   D. 20

6. Of two connected pulleys, the first pulley has a radius of 12 inches and rotates at 60 rpms; the second pulley has a diameter of 16 inches.
The speed of the second pulley is _____ rpms.   6._____

    A. 1000   B. 1020   C. 1040   D. 1080

7. If 16_{10} were converted to base 2, 8, and 16, the results would be _____ base 2, _____ base 8, and _____ base 16, respectively.   7._____

    A. 10000; 20; 10   B. 1000; 2000; 20
    C. 20000; 200; 20   D. 2000; 100; 10

8. Converting CAF_{16} to base 10 and base 8, the results would be _____ base 10 and _____ base 8, respectively.   8._____

    A. 2437; 2567   B. 3247; 6257
    C. 4327; 5267   D. 3427; 2657

9. Converting 101011001_2 to base 8, 10, and 16, the results would be _____ base 8, _____ base 10, and _____ base 16, respectively.　　9.____

   A.　135; 45; 59　　　　　　　　　　B.　567; 435; 259
   C.　315; 245; 135　　　　　　　　　D.　531; 345; 159

10. If 136_8 were converted to base 2, 10, and 16, the results would be _____ base 2, _____ base 10, and _____ base 16, respectively.　　10.____

   A.　001011110; 94, 5E　　　　　　　B.　010100110; 92; 10E
   C.　00100000; 90; 15E　　　　　　　D.　011001110; 96; 20E

11. It may be correctly stated that 1000 picofarads are equal to _____ microfarads.　　11.____

   A.　.0001　　　　B.　.001　　　　C.　.01　　　　D.　.1

12. If 5 megohms were converted to kohms, the result would be _____ kohms.　　12.____

   A.　1000　　　　B.　2000　　　　C.　4000　　　　D.　5000

13. 1 nanohenry would convert to _____ millihenries.　　13.____

   A.　.001　　　　B.　.0001　　　　C.　.00001　　　　D.　.0000001

14. If 7 milliamps were converted to microamps, the answer would be _____ microamps.　　14.____

   A.　7000　　　　B.　700　　　　C.　70　　　　D.　7

15. If two resistors are in parallel and are 100 ohms each, the total resistance is　　15.____

   A.　100　　　　B.　150　　　　C.　50　　　　D.　10

16. In reference to the circuit in Question 15, if the first resistor has 25 volts DC, (VDC) across it, the second resistor also has 25 VDC across it, and there are no other components in the circuit except for the power source, the total circuit voltage is _____ VDC.　　16.____

   A.　25　　　　B.　50　　　　C.　250　　　　D.　500

17. In reference to the circuit in Question 15, if the first resistor has 1 amp on it, and the second resistor also has 1 amp on it, the total circuit amperage is _____ amps.　　17.____

   A.　1　　　　B.　2　　　　C.　3　　　　D.　4

18. If two resistors are in series and are 100 ohms each, the total resistance is　　18.____

   A.　50　　　　B.　100　　　　C.　150　　　　D.　200

19. In reference to the circuit in Question 18, if the first resistor has 25 VDC across it and the second resistor also has 25 VDC across it, the total circuit voltage is　　19.____

   A.　50　　　　B.　100　　　　C.　200　　　　D.　500

20. In reference to the circuit in Question 18, if the first resistor has 1 amp across it and the second resistor also has 1 amp on it, the total circuit amperage is　　20.____

   A.　1　　　　B.　5　　　　C.　10　　　　D.　15 ·

21. Where two resistors are in parallel, one is 100 ohms and the other is 300 ohms.   21.____
    The total resistance is _____ ohms.

    A. 25   B. 35   C. 55   D. 75

22. Three resistors in series are 25 ohms, 50 ohms, and 75 ohms, respectively.   22.____
    The total resistance is _____ ohms.

    A. 25   B. 50   C. 100   D. 150

23. Two inductors are in parallel; the first is 50 henries and the second is also 50 henries.   23.____
    The total inductance is _____ henries.

    A. 25   B. 50   C. 55   D. 60

24. Two inductors are in series and the first is 50 henries; the second is 50 henries.   24.____
    The total inductance is _____ henries.

    A. 25   B. 50   C. 75   D. 100

25. Where two inductors are in parallel, the first is 100 henries and the second is 200 henries.   25.____
    The total inductance is _____ henries.

    A. 50   B. 75   C. 65   D. 100

KEY (CORRECT ANSWERS)

1.	C	6.	D	11.	B	16.	A	21.	D
2.	A	7.	A	12.	D	17.	B	22.	D
3.	B	8.	B	13.	D	18.	D	23.	A
4.	A	9.	D	14.	A	19.	A	24.	D
5.	B	10.	A	15.	C	20.	A	25.	B

TEST 2

DIRECTIONS: Each question or incomplete statement is followed by several suggested answers or completions. Select the one that BEST answers the question or completes the statement. *PRINT THE LETTER OF THE CORRECT ANSWER IN THE SPACE AT THE RIGHT.*

1. Two inductors are in series; the first inductor is 100 henries and the second is 200 henries.
   The total inductance is _____ henries.

   A. 200   B. 300   C. 400   D. 500

   1.____

2. Two capacitors are in parallel; each capacitor is 30 farads.
   The total capacitance is _____ farads.

   A. 60   B. 80   C. 100   D. 200

   2.____

3. Two capacitors are in series; each capacitor is 30 farads. The total capacitance is _____ farads.

   A. 10   B. 15   C. 20   D. 25

   3.____

4. Two capacitors are in parallel; the first is 50 farads and the second is 100 farads.
   The total capacitance is _____ farads.

   A. 50   B. 100   C. 125   D. 150

   4.____

5. Two capacitors are in series; the first is 50 farads and the second is 100 farads.
   The total capacitance is _____ farads.

   A. 33.333   B. 49.999   C. 13.333   D. 25.555

   5.____

6. A resistor's color codes are orange, blue, yellow, and gold, in that order.
   The value of the resistor is _____ kohms ± _____ %.

   A. 200; 2   B. 300; 4   C. 360; 5   D. 400; 7

   6.____

7. If a resistors color codes are red, black, and blue, the value of this resistor is _____ megohms ± _____ %.

   A. 20; 20   B. 40; 80   C. 30; 30   D. 50; 50

   7.____

8. If a resistor's color codes are gray, green, black, and silver, the resistor's value is _____ ohms ± _____ %.

   A. 55; 5   B. 75; 15   C. 85; 10   D. 100; 25

   8.____

9. One complete cycle of a sinewave takes 1000 microseconds. Its frequency is _____ hertz.

   A. 500   B. 1000   C. 2000   D. 5000

   9.____

10. If one complete cycle of a squarewave takes 5 microseconds, its frequency is _____ khertz.

    A. 200   B. 500   C. 700   D. 1000

    10.____

11. What is the PRT (pulse repetition time) of a 50 hertz (hz) sinewave? _____ milliseconds.

    A. 10   B. 20   C. 40   D. 60

    11._____

12. The PRT of a 20 khz sawtooth signal is _____ megahertz.

    A. 50   B. 100   C. 200   D. 500

    12._____

13. If a resistor measures 10 volts and 2 amps across it, the resistance is _____ ohms.

    A. 0   B. 2   C. 5   D. 10

    13._____

14. If a 30 ohm resistor measures 10 volts, the power consumed by the resistor is _____ watts.

    A. 3000   B. 5000   C. 6500   D. 7000

    14._____

15. If a 50 ohm resistor measures 4 amps across, the power consumed by it is _____ watts.

    A. 200   B. 400   C. 600   D. 800

    15._____

16. If a 100 ohm resistor measures 25 volts across, the current on it is _____ amps.

    A. .15   B. .25   C. .55   D. .65

    16._____

Questions 17-23.

DIRECTIONS: Questions 17 through 23 are to be answered on the basis of the following diagram.

SERIES CIRCUIT

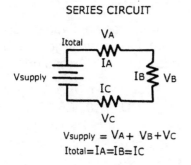

$V_{supply} = V_A + V_B + V_C$
$I_{total} = I_A = I_B = I_C$

PARALLEL CIRCUIT

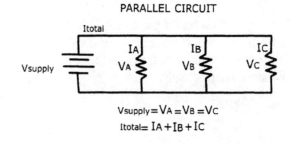

$V_{supply} = V_A = V_B = V_C$
$I_{total} = I_A + I_B + I_C$

17. In the series circuit above, if Vsupply = 100 VDC, resistor A is 10 ohms, resistor B is 50 ohms, and resistor C is 5 ohms, the total circuit current is _____ amps.

    A. 1.538   B. 1.267   C. 1.358   D. 1.823

    17._____

18. In the series circuit shown above, the current across each individual resistor is _____ amps.

    A. .5   B. 1.5   C. 2.5   D. 3.5

    18._____

19. In the series circuit shown above, the total power drawn by the circuit is _____ watts.   19._____

    A. 140.25   B. 150.75   C. 153.38   D. 173.38

20. In the series circuit shown above, the power drawn from each individual resistor is   20._____
    _____ , _____ , and _____ watts, respectively.

    A. 23.65; 118.27; 11.827   B. 17.567; 123.27; 11.27
    C. 18.627; 145.27; 12.27   D. 21.735; 116.87; 11.83

21. In the parallel circuit shown above, if Vsupply = 100 VDC, resistor A is 10 ohms, resistor   21._____
    B is 50 ohms, and resistor C is 5 ohms, the total circuit current is _____ amps.

    A. 21   B. 27   C. 32   D. 45

22. In the parallel circuit shown above, the total power drawn by the circuit is _____ watts.   22._____

    A. 1200   B. 2300   C. 2700   D. 3200

23. In the parallel circuit above, the power drawn by each individual resistor is _____ watts,   23._____
    respectively.

    A. 100; 200; 2000   B. 200; 400; 5000
    C. 300; 500; 750   D. 450; 600; 1500

24. On an 0-scope display, one cycle of a signal takes up 4 1/2 divisions and the peak-to-   24._____
    peak amplitude of the signal takes up 3 3/4 divisions.
    With the volts/division knob set on 5 volts and the time/division knob set to 5 microsec-
    onds, the peak-to-peak amplitude and the frequency of the signal are _____ volts and
    _____ khz, respectively.

    A. 15.75; 100   B. 22.5; 200
    C. 37.5; 350   D. 45.75; 570

25. If a signal that has a peak-to-peak amplitude of 15 volts and a frequency of 5 megaherz   25._____
    is to be observed on an 0-scope with one complete cycle shown, the time/division knob
    and volts/division knob should be set on _____ microseconds and _____ volts per
    division, respectively.

    A. .02; 2   B. .05; 4   C. .07; 3.5   D. 10; 7.5

KEY (CORRECT ANSWERS)

1. B	6. C	11. B	16. B	21. C
2. A	7. A	12. A	17. A	22. D
3. B	8. C	13. C	18. B	23. A
4. D	9. B	14. A	19. C	24. B
5. A	10. A	15. D	20. A	25. A

———

EXAMINATION SECTION
TEST 1

DIRECTIONS: Each question or incomplete statement is followed by several suggested answers or completions. Select the one that BEST answers the question or completes the statement. *PRINT THE LETTER OF THE CORRECT ANSWER IN THE SPACE AT THE RIGHT.*

Questions 1-6.

DIRECTIONS: Questions 1 through 6 are to be answered on the basis of the circuit diagram below. All switches are initially open.

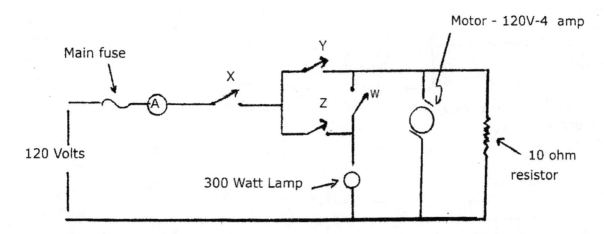

1. To light the 300 watt lamp, the following switches MUST be closed: 1._____

    A. X and Y   B. Y and Z   C. X and Z   D. X and W

2. If all of the switches W, X, Y, and Z are closed, the following will happen: 2._____

    A. The lamp will light and the motor will rotate
    B. The lamp will light and the motor will not rotate
    C. The lamp will not light and the motor will not rotate
    D. A short circuit will occur and the main fuse will blow

3. With 120 volts applied across the 10 ohm resistor, the current drawn by the resistor is   3._____
    _____ amp(s).

    A. 1/12   B. 1.2   C. 12   D. 1200

4. With 120 volts applied to the 10 ohm resistor, the power used by the resistor is _____   4._____
    kw.

    A. 1.44   B. 1.2   C. .144   D. .12

5. The current drawn by the 300 watt lamp when lighted should be APPROXIMATELY   5._____
    _____ amps.

    A. 2.5   B. 3.6   C. 25   D. 36

6. In the circuit shown, the symbol A is used to indicate a (n)   6.____

    A. ammeter   B. *and* circuit
    C. voltmeter   D. wattmeter

7. Of the following materials, the BEST conductor of electricity is   7.____

    A. iron   B. copper   C. aluminum   D. glass

8. The sum of 6'6", 5'9", and 2' 1 1/2" is   8.____

    A. 13'4 1/2"   B. 13'6 1/2"   C. 14'4 1/2"   D. 14'6 1/2"

9.   9.____

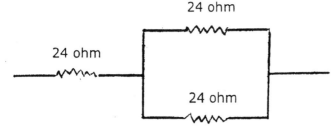

The equivalent resistance of the three resistors shown in the sketch above is _____ ohms.

    A. 8   B. 24   C. 36   D. 72

10.   10.____

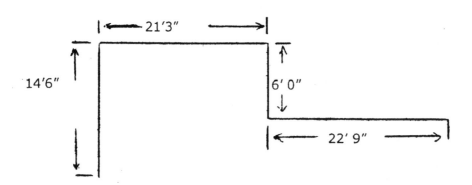

The TOTAL length of electrical conduit that must be run along the path shown on the diagram above is

    A. 63'8"   B. 64'6"   C. 65'6"   D. 66'8"

11. Of the following electrical devices, the one that is NOT normally used in direct current   11.____
electrical circuits is a (n)

    A. circuit breaker   B. double-pole switch
    C. transformer   D. inverter

12. The number of 120-volt light bulbs that should NORMALLY be connected in series   12.____
across a 600-volt electric line is

    A. 1   B. 2   C. 3   D. 5

13. Of the following motors, the one that does NOT have any brushes is the _____ motor.   13._____

   A. d.c. shunt   B. d.c. series
   C. squirrel cage induction   D. compound

14. Of the following materials, the one that is COMMONLY used as an electric heating ele-   14._____
   ment in an electric heater is

   A. zinc   B. brass
   C. terne plate   D. nichrome

Questions 15-25.

DIRECTIONS: Questions 15 through 25 are to be answered on the basis of the instruments
               listed below. Each instrument is listed with an identifying number in front of it.

   1 - Hygrometer   9 - Vernier caliper
   2 - Ammeter   10 - Wire gage
   3 - Voltmeter   11 - 6-foot folding rule
   4 - Wattmeter   12 - Architect's scale
   5 - Megger   13 - Planimeter
   6 - Oscilloscope   14 - Engineer's scale
   7 - Frequency meter   15 - Ohmmeter
   8 - Micrometer

15. The instrument that should be used to accurately measure the resistance of a 4,700 ohm   15._____
   resistor is Number

   A. 3   B. 4   C. 7   D. 15

16. To measure the current in an electrical circuit, the instrument that should be used is   16._____
   Number

   A. 2   B. 7   C. 8   D. 15

17. To measure the insulation resistance of a rubber-covered electrical cable, the instrument   17._____
   that should be used is Number

   A. 4   B. 5   C. 8   D. 15

18. An AC motor is hooked up to a power distribution box.   18._____
   In order to check the voltage at the motor terminals, the instrument that should be
   used is Number

   A. 2   B. 3   C. 4   D. 7

19. To measure the shaft diameter of a motor accurately to one-thousandth of an inch, the   19._____
   instrument that should be used is Number

   A. 8   B. 10   C. 11   D. 14

20. The instrument that should be used to determine whether 25 Hz. or 60 Hz. is present in   20._____
   an electrical circuit is Number

   A. 4   B. 5   C. 7   D. 8

21. Of the following, the PROPER instrument to use to determine the diameter of the con-ductor of a piece of electrical hook-up wire is Number   21.____

    A. 10   B. 11   C. 12   D. 14

22. The amount of electrical power being used in a balanced three-phase circuit should be measured with Number   22.____

    A. 2   B. 3   C. 4   D. 5

23. The electrical wave form at a given point in an electronic circuit can be observed with Number   23.____

    A. 2   B. 3   C. 6   D. 7

24. The PROPER instrument to use for measuring the width of a door is Number   24.____

    A. 11   B. 12   C. 13   D. 14

25. A one-inch hole with a tolerance of plus or minus three-thousandths is reamed in a steel block.
The PROPER instrument to use to accurately check the diameter of the hole is Number   25.____

    A. 8   B. 9   C. 11   D. 14

KEY (CORRECT ANSWERS)

1.	C	11.	C
2.	A	12.	D
3.	C	13.	C
4.	A	14.	D
5.	A	15.	D
6.	A	16.	A
7.	B	17.	B
8.	C	18.	B
9.	C	19.	A
10.	B	20.	C

21.	A
22.	C
23.	C
24.	A
25.	B

TEST 2

DIRECTIONS: Each question or incomplete statement is followed by several suggested answers or completions. Select the one that BEST answers the question or completes the statement. *PRINT THE LETTER OF THE CORRECT ANSWER IN THE SPACE AT THE RIGHT.*

1. The number of conductors required to connect a 3-phase delta connected heater bank to an electric power panel board is

   A. 2   B. 3   C. 4   D. 5   1.____

2. Of the following, the wire size that is MOST commonly used for branch lighting circuits in homes is _____ A.W.G.

   A. #12   B. #8   C. #6   D. #4   2.____

3. When installing electrical circuits, the tool that should be used to pull wire through a conduit is a

   A. mandrel   B. snake
   C. rod   D. pulling iron   3.____

4. Of the following AC voltages, the LOWEST voltage that a neon test lamp can detect is _____ volts.

   A. 6   B. 12   C. 80   D. 120   4.____

5. Of the following, the BEST procedure to use when storing tools that are subject to rusting is to

   A. apply a thin coating of soap onto the tools
   B. apply a light coating of oil to the tools
   C. wrap the tools in clean cheesecloth
   D. place the tools in a covered container   5.____

6. If a 3 1/2 inch long nail is required to nail wood framing members together, the nail size to use should be

   A. 2d   B. 4d   C. 16d   D. 60d   6.____

7. Of the four motors listed below, the one that can operate only on alternating current is a(n) _____ motor.

   A. series   B. shunt
   C. compound   D. induction   7.____

8. The sum of 1/3 + 2/5 + 5/6 is

   A. 1 17/30   B. 1 3/5   C. 1 15/24   D. 1 5/6   8.____

9. Of the following instruments, the one that should be used to measure the state of charge of a lead-acid storage battery is a(n)

   A. ammeter   B. ohmmeter
   C. hydrometer   D. thermometer   9.____

10. If three 1 1/2 volt dry cell batteries are wired in series, the TOTAL voltage provided by the three batteries is _____ volts.   10._____

    A.   1.5   B.   3   C.   4.5   D.   6.0

11. Taking into account time and one-half payment for time over 40 hours of work, the gross pay of an employee who works 43 hours in a week at a rate of pay of $10.68 per hour is   11._____

    A. $427.20   B. $459.24   C. $475.26   D. $491.28

12. The sum of 0.365 + 3.941 + 10.676 + 0.784 is   12._____

    A.   13.766   B.   15.666   C.   15.756   D.   15.766

13. In order to transmit mechanical power between two rotating shafts at right angles to each other, two gears are used. Of the following, the type of gears that should be used are _____ gears.   13._____

    A.   herringbone   B.   spur
    C.   bevel   D.   rack and pinion

14. To properly ground the service electrical equipment in a building, a ground connection should be made to _____ the building.   14._____

    A.   the waste or soil line leaving
    B.   the vent line going to the exterior of
    C.   any steel beam in
    D.   the cold water line entering

15. The area of the triangle shown at the right is _____ square inches.   15._____
    A.   120
    B.   240
    C.   360
    D.   480

Questions 16-25.

DIRECTIONS: Questions 16 through 25 are to be answered on the basis of the tools shown on the next page. The tools are not shown to scale. Each tool is shown with an identifying number alongside it.

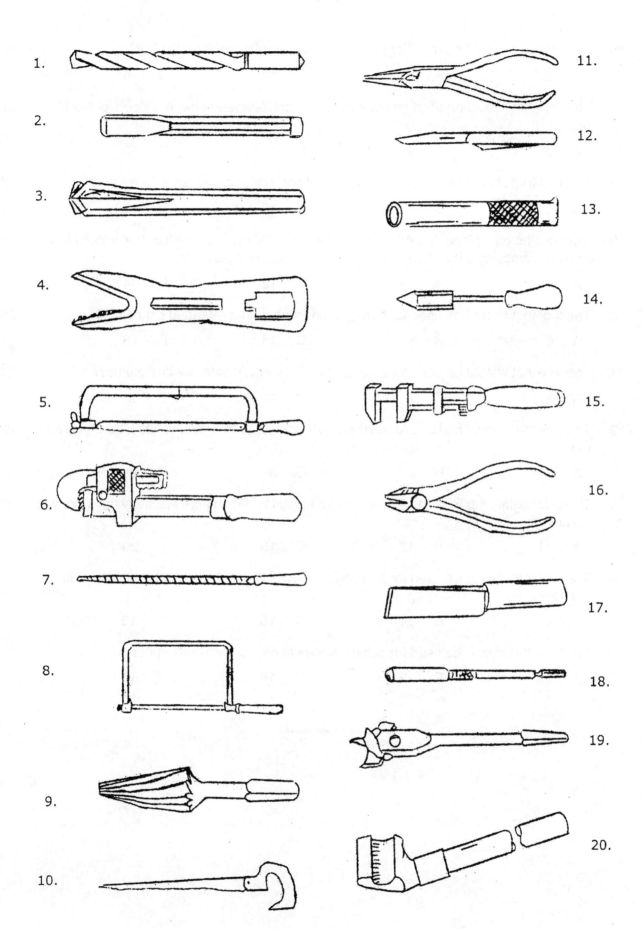

1.

2.

3.

4.

5.

6.

7.

8.

9.

10.

11.

12.

13.

14.

15.

16.

17.

18.

19.

20.

16. The tool that should be used for cutting thin wall steel conduit is Number   16.____
     A. 5   B. 8   C. 10   D. 16

17. The tool that should be used for cutting a 1 7/8 inch diameter hole in a wood joist is Number   17.____
     A. 3   B. 9   C. 14   D. 19

18. The tool that should be used for soldering splices in electrical wire is Number   18.____
     A. 3   B. 7   C. 13   D. 14

19. After cutting off a piece of 3/4 inch diameter electrical conduit, the tool that should be used for removing a burr from the inside of the conduit is Number   19.____
     A. 9   B. 11   C. 12   D. 14

20. The tool that should be used for turning a coupling onto a threaded conduit is Number   20.____
     A. 6   B. 11   C. 15   D. 16

21. The tool that should be used for cutting wood lathing in plaster walls is Number   21.____
     A. 5   B. 7   C. 10   D. 12

22. The tool that should be used for drilling a 3/8 inch diameter hole in a steel beam is Number   22.____
     A. 1   B. 2   C. 3   D. 9

23. Of the following, the BEST tool to use for stripping insulation from electrical hook-up wire is Number   23.____
     A. 11   B. 12   C. 15   D. 20

24. The tool that should be used for bending an electrical wire around a terminal post is Number   24.____
     A. 4   B. 11   C. 15   D. 16

25. The tool that should be used for cutting electrical hookup wire is Number   25.____
     A. 5   B. 12   C. 16   D. 17

———————

KEY (CORRECT ANSWERS)

1.	B	11.	C
2.	A	12.	D
3.	B	13.	C
4.	C	14.	D
5.	B	15.	A
6.	C	16.	A
7.	D	17.	D
8.	A	18.	D
9.	C	19.	A
10.	C	20.	A

21.	C
22.	A
23.	B
24.	B
25.	C

TEST 3

DIRECTIONS: Each question or incomplete statement is followed by several suggested answers or completions. Select the one that BEST answers the question or completes the statement. *PRINT THE LETTER OF THE CORRECT ANSWER IN THE SPACE AT THE RIGHT.*

1. An electric circuit has current flowing through it. The panel board switch feeding the circuit is opened, causing arcing across the switch contacts.
   Generally, this arcing is caused by

   A. a lack of energy storage in the circuit
   B. electrical energy stored by a capacitor
   C. electrical energy stored by a resistor
   D. magnetic energy induced by an inductance

   1.____

2. MOST filter capacitors in radios have a capacity rating given in

   A. microvolts   B. milliamps
   C. millihenries   D. microfarads

   2.____

3. Of the following, the electrical wire size that is COMMONLY used for telephone circuits is _____ A.W.G.

   A. #6   B. #10   C. #12   D. #22

   3.____

Questions 4-9.

DIRECTIONS: Questions 4 through 9 are to be answered on the basis of the electrical circuit diagram shown below, where letters are used to identify various circuit components.

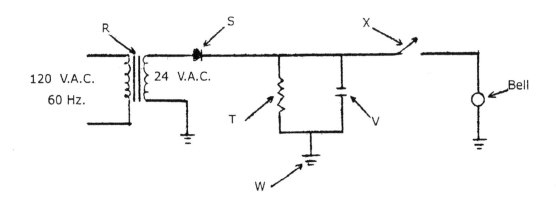

4. The device indicated by the letter R is a

   A. capacitor   B. converter
   C. resistor   D. transformer

   4.____

5. The device indicated by the letter S is a

   A. transistor   B. diode
   C. thermistor   D. directional relay

   5.____

6. The devices indicated by the letters T and V are used together to _____ components of the secondary current.

   A. reduce the AC   B. reduce the DC
   C. transform the AC   D. invert the AC

   6.____

7. The letter W points to a standard electrical symbol for a

   A. wire   B. ground
   C. terminal   D. lightning arrestor

   7.____

8. Closing switch X will apply the following type of voltage to the bell:

   A. 60 Hz. AC   B. DC
   C. pulsating AC   D. 120 Hz. AC

   8.____

9. The circuit shown contains a _____ rectifier.

   A. mercury-arc   B. full-wave
   C. bridge   D. half-wave

   9.____

10. A bolt specified as 1/4-28 means the following:
    The

    A. bolt is 1/4 inch in diameter and has 28 threads per inch
    B. bolt is 1/4 inch in diameter and is 2.8 inches long
    C. bolt is 1/4 inch long and has 28 threads
    D. threaded portion of the bolt is 1/4 inch long and has 28 threads per inch

    10.____

11. When cutting 0.045-inch thickness sheet metal, it is BEST to use a hacksaw blade that has _____ teeth per inch.

    A. 7   B. 12   C. 18   D. 32

    11.____

12. To accurately tighten a bolt to 28 foot-pounds, it is BEST to use a(n) _____ wrench.

    A. pipe   B. open end   C. box   D. torque

    12.____

13. When bending a 2-inch diameter conduit, the CORRECT tool to use is a

    A. hickey   B. pipe wrench
    C. hydraulic bender   D. stock and die

    13.____

14. When soldering two #20 A.W.G. copper wires together to form a splice, the solder that SHOULD be used is _____ solder.

    A. acid-core   B. solid-core
    C. rosin-core   D. liquid

    14.____

15. A bathroom heating unit draws 10 amperes at 115 volts.
    The hot resistance of the heating unit should be _____ ohms.

    A. .08   B. 8   C. 11.5   D. 1150

    15.____

16. Of the following materials, the one that is NOT suitable as an electrical insulator is

    A. glass   B. mica   C. rubber   D. platinum

    16.____

17. An air conditioning unit is rated at 1000 watts. The unit is run for 10 hours per day, five days per week.
    If the cost for electrical energy is 5 cents per kilowatt-hour, the weekly cost for electricity should be

    A. 25¢   B. 50¢   C. $2.50   D. $25.00

17.____

18. If a fuse is protecting the circuit of a 15 ohm electric heater and it is designed to blow out at a current exceeding 10 amperes, the MAXIMUM voltage from among the following that should be applied across the terminals of the heater is _____ volts.

    A. 110   B. 120   C. 160   D. 600

18.____

19. Before opening a pneumatic hose connection, it is important to remove pressure from the hose line PRIMARILY to avoid

    A. losing air
    B. personal injury
    C. damage to the hose connection
    D. a build-up of pressure in the air compressor

19.____

20. If the scale on a shop drawing is 1/4 inch to the foot, then a part which measures 3 3/8 inches long on the drawing has an ACTUAL length of _____ feet _____ inches.

    A. 12; 6   B. 13; 6   C. 13; 9   D. 14; 9

20.____

21. The function that is USUALLY performed by a motor controller is to

    A. start and stop a motor
    B. protect a motor from a short circuit
    C. prevent bearing failure of a motor
    D. control the brush wear in a motor

21.____

22. Of the following galvanized sheet metal electrical outlet boxes, the one that is NOT a commonly used size is the _____ box.

    A. 4" square   B. 4" octagonal
    C. 4" x 2 1/8"   D. 4" x 1"

22.____

23. When soldering a transistor into a circuit, it is MOST important to protect the transistor from

    A. the application of an excess of rosin flux
    B. excessive heat
    C. the application of an excess of solder
    D. too much pressure

23.____

24. When installing BX type cable, it is important to protect the wires in the cable from the cut ends of the armored sheath.
    The APPROVED method of providing this protection is to

    A. use a fiber or plastic insulating bushing
    B. file the cut ends of the sheath smooth
    C. use a connector where the cable enters a junction box
    D. tie the wires into an Underwriter's knot

24.____

25. While lifting a heavy piece of equipment off the floor, a person should NOT   25.____

    A. twist his body
    B. grasp it firmly
    C. maintain a solid footing on the ground
    D. bend his knees

26. It is important that metal cabinets and panels that house electrical equipment should be   26.____
grounded PRIMARILY in order to

    A. prevent short circuits from occurring
    B. keep all circuits at ground potential
    C. minimize shock hazards
    D. reduce the effects of electrolytic corrosion

27. A foreman explains a technical procedure to a new employee. If the employee does not   27.____
understand the instructions he has received, it would be BEST if he were to

    A. follow the procedure as best he could
    B. ask the foreman to explain it to him again
    C. avoid following the procedure
    D. ask the foreman to give him other work

28. Of the following, the BEST connectors to use when mounting an electrical panel box   28.____
directly onto a concrete wall are

    A. threaded studs   B. machine screws
    C. lag screws   D. expansion bolts

29. Of the following, the BEST instrument to use to measure the small gap between relay   29.____
contacts is

    A. a micrometer   B. a feeler gage
    C. inside calipers   D. a plug gage

30. A POSSIBLE result of mounting a 40 ampere fuse in a fuse box for a circuit requiring a   30.____
20 ampere fuse is that the 40 ampere fuse may

    A. provide twice as much protection to the circuit from overloads
    B. blow more easily than the smaller fuse due to an overload
    C. cause serious damage to the circuit from an overload
    D. reduce power consumption in the circuit

KEY (CORRECT ANSWERS)

1.	D		16.	D
2.	D		17.	C
3.	D		18.	B
4.	D		19.	B
5.	B		20.	B
6.	A		21.	A
7.	B		22.	D
8.	B		23.	B
9.	D		24.	A
10.	A		25.	A
11.	D		26.	C
12.	D		27.	B
13.	C		28.	D
14.	C		29.	B
15.	C		30.	C

EXAMINATION SECTION
TEST 1

DIRECTIONS: Each question or incomplete statement is followed by several suggested answers or completions. Select the one that BEST answers the question or completes the statement. *PRINT THE LETTER OF THE CORRECT ANSWER IN THE SPACE AT THE RIGHT.*

Questions 1-8.

DIRECTIONS: Questions 1 through 8 involve tests on the fuse box arrangement shown below. All tests are to be performed with a neon tester or a lamp test bank consisting of two 6-watt, 120-volt lamps connected in series. Do not make any assumptions about the conditions of the circuits. Draw your conclusions only from the information obtained with the neon tester or the two-lamp test bank, applied to the circuits as called for.

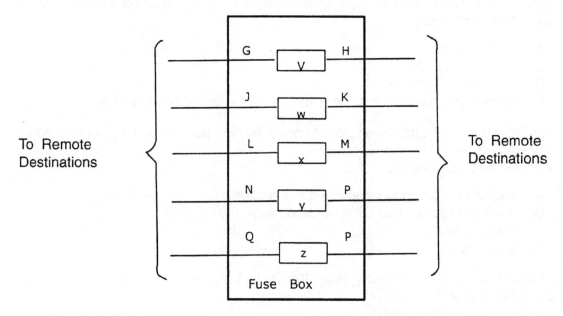

1. The two lamp test bank is placed from point G to joint J, and both lamps light. One of the lamps is momentarily removed from its socket; during that instant, the other lamp in the series-connected test bank should

    A. go dark
    B. get dimmer
    C. remain at same brightness
    D. get brighter

1.____

2. The test bank with two 60-watt, 120-volt lamps in series should be used on circuits with

    A. wattages only from 60 to 120 watts
    B. wattages only from 0 to 120 watts
    C. voltages only from 120 to 240 volts
    D. voltages only from 0 to 240 volts

2.____

3. The neon tester is placed from point G to point J and only one-half of the neon tester lights.
It should be concluded that

    A. half of the tester has gone bad
    B. a wire has become disconnected in the circuit
    C. the voltage is AC
    D. the voltage is DC

3.____

4. If both lamps in the test bank light when placed directly across one of the above fuses, it should be concluded that

    A. the fuse is good
    B. the fuse is blown
    C. the fuse is overrated
    D. further tests have to be made to determine the condition of the fuse

4.____

5. If the lamp test bank does not light when placed directly across one of the above fuses, it should be concluded that

    A. the fuse is good
    B. the fuse is blown
    C. the fuse is overrated
    D. further tests have to be made to determine the condition of the fuse

5.____

6. The lamp test bank lights when placed from point G to point J but does not light when placed from point H to point J.
It should be concluded that

    A. the wire to point H has become disconnected
    B. the wire to point J has become disconnected
    C. fuse v is bad
    D. fuse w is bad

6.____

7. The lamp test bank lights when placed from point L to point N but does not light when placed from point M to point P.
It should be concluded that

    A. both fuses x and y are bad
    B. either fuse x or fuse y is bad or both are bad
    C. both fuses x and y are good
    D. these tests do not indicate the condition of any fuse

7.____

8. The lamp test bank is placed from point L to point N, then from N to point Q, and finally from point L to point Q. In each case, both lamps light to full brightness.
It should be concluded that points L, N, and Q have

    A. three-phase, 120 volts, AC, line-to-line
    B. plus and minus 120 volts, DC
    C. three-phase, 208 volts, AC
    D. plus and minus 240 volts, DC

8.____

9. The resistance of a copper wire to the flow of electricity _____ as the _____ of the wire _____.

    A. increases; diameter; increases
    B. decreases; diameter; decreases
    C. decreases; length; increases
    D. increases; length; increases

      9.____

10. Where galvanized steel conduit is used, the PRIMARY purpose of the galvanizing is to

    A. increase mechanical strength
    B. retard rusting
    C. provide a good surface for painting
    D. provide good electrical contact for grounding

      10.____

11. The lamps used for station and tunnel lighting in subways are generally operated at slightly less than their rated voltage.
The LOGICAL reason for this is to

    A. prevent overloading of circuits
    B. increase the life of the lamps
    C. decrease glare
    D. obtain a more even distribution of light

      11.____

12. The CORRECT method of measuring the power taken by an AC electric motor is to use a

    A. wattmeter   B. voltmeter and an ammeter
    C. power factor meter   D. tachometer

      12.____

13. Wood ladders should NOT be painted because the paint may

    A. deteriorate the wood   B. make ladders slippery
    C. be inflammable   D. cover cracks or defects

      13.____

14. Goggles would be LEAST necessary when

    A. recharging soda-acid fire extinguishers
    B. chipping stone
    C. putting electrolyte into an Edison battery
    D. scraping rubber insulation from a wire

      14.____

15. The number and type of precautions to be taken on a job generally depend LEAST on the

    A. nature of the job
    B. length of time the job is expected to last
    C. kind of tools and materials being used
    D. location of the work

      15.____

16. When training workers in the use of tools and equipment, safety precautions related to their use should be FIRST mentioned

    A. in the introductory training session before the workers begin to use the equipment or tools
    B. during training sessions when workers practice operating the tools or equipment

      16.____

C. after the workers are qualified to use the equipment in their daily tasks
D. when an agency safety bulletin related to the tools and equipment is received

17. Artificial respiration should be started immediately on a man who has suffered an electric shock if he is   17.____

    A. *unconscious* and breathing
    B. *unconscious* and not breathing
    C. *conscious* and in a daze
    D. *conscious* and badly burned

18. The fuse of a certain circuit has blown and is replaced with a fuse of the same rating which also blows when the switch is closed.
In this case,   18.____

    A. a fuse of higher current rating should be used
    B. a fuse of higher voltage rating should be used
    C. the fuse should be temporarily replaced by a heavy piece of wire
    D. the circuit should be checked

19. Operating an incandescent electric light bulb at less than its rated voltage will result in   19.____

    A. shorter life and brighter light
    B. longer life and dimmer light
    C. brighter light and longer life
    D. dimmer light and shorter life

20. In order to control a lamp from two different positions, it is necessary to use   20.____

    A. two single pole switches
    B. one single pole switch and one four-way switch
    C. two three-way switches
    D. one single pole switch and one four-way switch

21. One method of testing fuses is to connect a pair of test lamps in the circuit in such a manner that the test lamp will light up if the fuse is good and will remain dark if the fuse is bad. In the illustration at the right, 1 and 2 are fuses.
In order to test if fuse 1 is bad, test lamps should be connected between   21.____
    A. A and B
    B. B and D
    C. A and D
    D. C and B

22. The PRINCIPAL reason for the grounding of electrical equipment and circuits is to   22.____

    A. prevent short circuits   B. insure safety from shock
    C. save power   D. increase voltage

23. An interlock is generally installed on electronic equipment to
        A.   prevent loss of power
        B.   maintain VHF frequencies
        C.   keep the vacuum tubes lit
        D.   prevent electric shock during maintenance operations
23.____

24. A flame should not be used to inspect the electrolyte level in a lead-acid battery because the battery cells give off highly flammable
24.____

        A.   hydrogen   B.   lead oxide
        C.   lithium   D.   xenon

25. The purpose of the third prong in a three-prong male electric plug used in a 120 volt circuit is to
25.____

        A.   make a firm connection   B.   strengthen the plug
        C.   ground to prevent shock   D.   act as a transducer

---

KEY (CORRECT ANSWERS)

1.	A		11.	B
2.	D		12.	A
3.	D		13.	D
4.	B		14.	D
5.	D		15.	B
6.	C		16.	A
7.	B		17.	B
8.	C		18.	D
9.	D		19.	B
10.	B		20.	C

21.	C
22.	B
23.	D
24.	A
25.	C

TEST 2

DIRECTIONS: Each question or incomplete statement is followed by several suggested answers or completions. Select the one that BEST answers the question or completes the statement. *PRINT THE LETTER OF THE CORRECT ANSWER IN THE SPACE AT THE RIGHT.*

1. The BEST procedure to follow when replacing a blown fuse is to   1._____

    A. immediately replace it with the same size fuse
    B. immediately replace it with a larger size fuse
    C. immediately replace it with a smaller size fuse
    D. correct the cause of the fuse failure and replace it with the correct size

2. The amperage rating of the fuse to be used in an electrical circuit is determined by the   2._____

    A. size of the connected load
    B. size of the wire in the circuit
    C. voltage of the circuit
    D. ambient temperature

3. In a 208 volt, three-phase, 4 wire circuit, the voltage, in volts, from any line to the grounded neutral is APPROXIMATELY   3._____

    A. 208   B. 150   C. 120   D. zero

4. The device commonly used to change an AC voltage to a DC voltage is called a   4._____

    A. transformer   B. rectifier
    C. relay   D. capacitor or condenser

5. Where conduit enters a knock-out in an outlet box, it should be provided with a   5._____

    A. bushing on the inside and locknut on the outside
    B. locknut on the inside and bushing on the outside
    C. union on the outside and a nipple on the inside
    D. nipple on the outside and a union on the inside

6. The electric circuit to a ten kilowatt electric hot water heater which is automatically controlled by an aquastat will also require a   6._____

    A. transistor   B. choke coil
    C. magnetic contactor   D. limit switch

7. An electric power consumption meter USUALLY indicates the power used in   7._____

    A. watts   B. volt-hours
    C. amperes   D. kilowatt-hours

8. Of the following sizes of copper wire, the one which can SAFELY carry the greatest amount of amperes is   8._____

    A. 14 ga. stranded   B. 12 ga. stranded
    C. 12 ga. solid   D. 10 ga. solid

9. If a 110 volt lamp were used on a 220 volt circuit, the   9._____

    A. fuse would burn out   B. lamp would burn out
    C. line would overheat   D. lamp would flicker

10. The material which is LEAST likely to be found in use as the outer covering of rubber   10._____
insulated wires or cables is

    A. cotton   B. varnished cambric
    C. lead   D. neoprene

11. In measuring to determine the size of a stranded insulated conductor, the PROPER   11._____
place to use the wire gauge is on

    A. the insulation
    B. the outer covering
    C. the stranded conductor
    D. one strand of the conductor

12. Rubber insulation on an electrical conductor would MOST quickly be damaged by contin-   12._____
uous contact with

    A. acid   B. water   C. oil   D. alkali

13. If a fuse clip becomes hot under normal circuit load, the MOST probable cause is that the   13._____

    A. clip makes poor contact with the fuse ferrule
    B. circuit wires are too small
    C. current rating of the fuse is too high
    D. voltage rating of the fuse is too low

14. If the input to a 10 to 1 step-down transformer is 15 amperes at 2400 volts, the second-   14._____
ary output would be NEAREST to _____ amperes at _____ volts.

    A. 1.5; 24,000   B. 150; 240
    C. 1.5; 240   D. 150; 24,000

15. In a two-wire electrical system, the color of the wire which is grounded is USUALLY   15._____

    A. white   B. red   C. black   D. green

16. It is generally recommended that wooden ladders be kept coated with a suitable protec-   16._____
tive coating.
The one of the following which is NOT a suitable protective coating is

    A. clear lacquer   B. clear varnish
    C. linseed oil   D. paint

17. The tool you should use to mend metal by soldering is   17._____

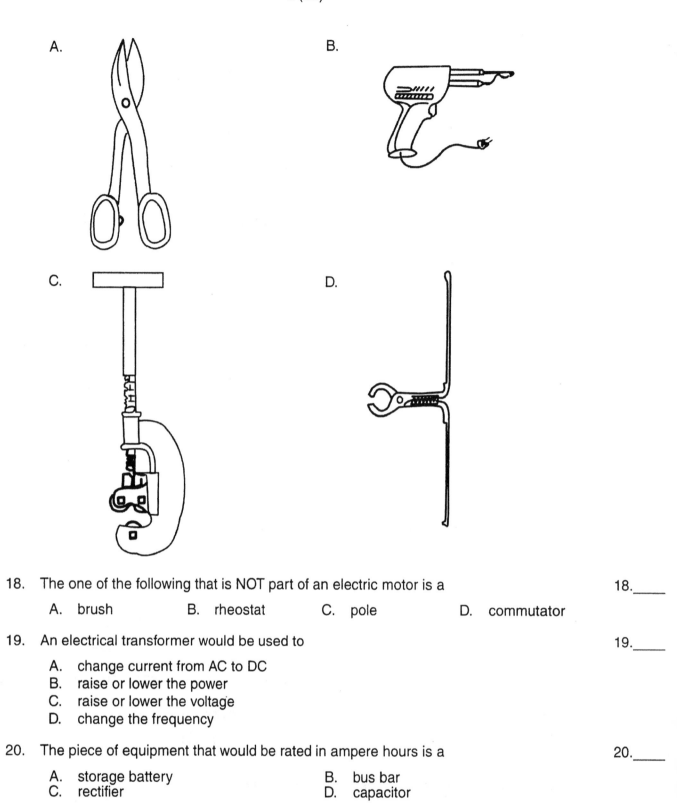

A.

B.

C.

D.

18. The one of the following that is NOT part of an electric motor is a   18.____

    A. brush   B. rheostat   C. pole   D. commutator

19. An electrical transformer would be used to   19.____

    A. change current from AC to DC
    B. raise or lower the power
    C. raise or lower the voltage
    D. change the frequency

20. The piece of equipment that would be rated in ampere hours is a   20.____

    A. storage battery   B. bus bar
    C. rectifier   D. capacitor

21. A ballast is a necessity in a(n)   21.·____

    A. motor generator set
    B. fluorescent lighting system
    C. oil circuit breaker
    D. synchronous converter

22. The power factor in an AC circuit is on when   22._____

    A. no current is flowing
    B. the voltage at the source is a minimum
    C. the voltage and current are in phase
    D. there is no load

23. Neglecting the internal resistance in the battery, the current flowing through the battery shown at the right is _____ amp.   23._____

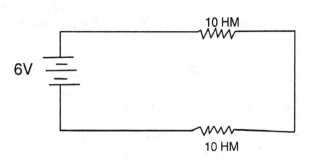

    A. 3
    B. 6
    C. 9
    D. 12

24. Using a fuse with a LARGER rated capacity than that of the circuit is   24._____

    A. *advisable;* such use prevents the fuse from blowing
    B. *advisable;* larger capacity fuses last longer than smaller capacity fuses
    C. *inadvisable;* larger capacity fuses are more expensive than smaller capacity fuses
    D. *inadvisable;* such use may cause a fire

25. You can MOST easily tell when a screw-in type fuse has blown because the center of the strip of metal in the fuse is   25._____

    A. broken   B. visible
    C. nicked   D. cool to the touch

KEY (CORRECT ANSWERS)

1.	D		11.	D
2.	B		12.	C
3.	C		13.	A
4.	B		14.	B
5.	A		15.	A
6.	C		16.	D
7.	D		17.	B
8.	D		18.	B
9.	B		19.	C
10.	B		20.	A

21.	B
22.	C
23.	A
24.	D
25.	A

TEST 3

DIRECTIONS: Each question or incomplete statement is followed by several suggested answers or completions. Select the one that BEST answers the question or completes the statement. *PRINT THE LETTER OF THE CORRECT ANSWER IN THE SPACE AT THE RIGHT.*

1. The ordinary single-pole flush wall type switch must be connected   1.____

    A. across the line
    B. in the hot conductor
    C. in the grounded conductor
    D. in the white conductor

2. A DC shunt motor runs in the wrong direction.   2.____
    This fault can be CORRECTED by

    A. reversing the connections of both the field and the armature
    B. interchanging the connections of either main or auxiliary windings
    C. interchanging the connections to either the field or the armature windings
    D. interchanging the connections to the line of the power leads

3. The MOST common type of motor that can be used with both AC and DC sources is the   3.____
    _____ motor.

    A. compound   B. repulsion   C. series   D. shunt

4. A fluorescent fixture in a new building has been in use for several months without trouble.   4.____
    Recently, the ends of the fluorescent lamp have remained lighted when the light was switched off.
    The BEST way to clear up this trouble is to replace the

    A. lamp   B. ballast   C. starter   D. sockets

5. A ballast is a part of a(n)   5.____

    A. fluorescent light fixture
    B. electric motor
    C. doorbell circuit
    D. incandescent light fixture

6. Most of the lighting circuits in buildings operate on _____ volts.   6.____
    A. 6   B. 12   C. 120   D. 208

7. An ordinary wall switch called a *silent switch* contains a liquid called   7.____
    A. water   B. mercury   C. oil   D. naptha

8. The rating of the circuit breaker in a lighting circuit is determined by the   8.____

    A. load connected to the circuit
    B. current carrying capacity of the wire
    C. ambient temperature
    D. length of the wire

9. One ADVANTAGE of rubber insulation is that it 9.____

    A. does not deteriorate with age
    B. is able to withstand high temperatures
    C. does not absorb much moisture
    D. is not damaged by oil

10. The SIMPLEST device for interrupting an overloaded electrical circuit is a 10.____

    A. fuse   B. relay
    C. capacitor   D. choke coil

11. Electric service meters are read in 11.____

    A. kilowatt hours   B. electrons
    C. amperes   D. volts

12. The device used to reduce the voltage of an electric circuit is the 12.____

    A. voltmeter   B. fuse
    C. circuit breaker   D. transformer

13. Ordinary light bulbs are USUALLY rated in 13.____

    A. watts   B. ohms   C. amperes   D. filaments

14. The electric plug on a scrubbing machine should be plugged into a 14.____

    A. light socket   B. wall outlet
    C. fuse receptacle   D. dimmer switch

15. The device which should be used to connect the output shaft of an electric motor to the input shaft of a centrifugal pump is the 15.____

    A. flexible coupling   B. petcock
    C. alemite fitting   D. clutch

16. When comparing a 60 watt yellow bulb with a 60 watt clear bulb, it can be said that they BOTH 16.____

    A. give the same amount of light
    B. use the same amount of power
    C. will burn for at least 60 hours
    D. will burn for at least 60 days

17. The output capacity of an electric motor is USUALLY rated in 17.____

    A. kilowatts   B. horsepower
    C. percent   D. cubic feet

18. A fuse will burn out whenever it is subjected to excessive 18.____

    A. resistance   B. voltage
    C. current   D. capacitance

19. The one of the following that is BEST to use to smooth a commutator is 19.____

    A. Number 1/0 emery cloth   B. Number 00 sandpaper
    C. Number 2 steel wool   D. a safe edge file

20. The electric service that is provided to MOST schools in the city is NOMINALLY _____   20.____
volt- _____ phase - _____ wire - _____ volts to ground.

     A.   208; 3; 4; 120   B.   208; 3; 3; 208
     C.   220; 2; 3; 110   D.   440; 3; 4; 240

21. All the fuses in an electrical panel are good but the clips on the fuse in circuit No. 1 are   21.____
much hotter than the clips of the other fuses.
Of the following, the MOST likely cause of this condition is that

     A.   circuit No. 1 is greatly overloaded
     B.   circuit No. 1 is carrying much less than rated load
     C.   the room temperature is abnormally high
     D.   the fuse in circuit No. 1 is very loose in its clips

22. Before putting two DC engine generators on the line in parallel, it is USUALLY necessary   22.____
to

     A.   adjust the speeds so that both are running at exactly the same speed
     B.   adjust the loads so that each machine will take its proportionate share
     C.   adjust the field of the incoming unit
     D.   lower the line voltage

23. Of the following, the BEST type of AC motor to use for direct connection to a timing   23.____
device which must be very accurate is a _____ motor.

     A.   synchronous   B.   squirrel cage
     C.   wound rotor   D.   single phase capacitor

24. In running temporary electric wiring for a display requiring the use of 30 incandescent 50-   24.____
watt lamps at the usual lighting voltage, the two main 120V loads supplying this load
would carry MOST NEARLY _____ amps.

     A.   23.9   B.   12.5   C.   17.8   D.   9.5

25. The BEST of the following tools to use for cutting off a piece of single conductor #6 rub-   25.____
ber insulated lead covered cable is a

     A.   pair of electrician's pliers
     B.   hacksaw
     C.   hammer and cold chisel
     D.   lead knife

KEY (CORRECT ANSWERS)

1.	B		11.	A
2.	C		12.	D
3.	C		13.	A
4.	C		14.	B
5.	A		15.	A
6.	C		16.	B
7.	B		17.	B
8.	B		18.	C
9.	C		19.	B
10.	A		20.	A

21.	D
22.	C
23.	A
24.	B
25.	B

TEST 4

DIRECTIONS: Each question or incomplete statement is followed by several suggested answers or completions. Select the one that BEST answers the question or completes the statement. *PRINT THE LETTER OF THE CORRECT ANSWER IN THE SPACE AT THE RIGHT.*

1. An indication that a fluorescent lamp in a fixture should be replaced is   1.____

    A. humming in the fixture
    B. the ends of the lamp remain black when the lamp is lit
    C. poor or slow starting
    D. the lamp does not shut off each time the OFF button is pressed

2. Asbestos is used as a covering on electrical wires to provide protection from   2.____

    A. high voltage   B. high temperatures
    C. water damage   D. electrolysis

3. Many electric power tools, such as drills, have a third conductor in the line cord which   3.____
   should be connected to a grounded part of the power receptacle.
   The reason for this is to

    A. have a spare wire in case one power wire should break
    B. strengthen the power lead so that it cannot be easily damaged
    C. protect the user of the tool from electrical shocks
    D. allow use of the tool for extended periods of time without overheating

4. A riser diagram is an electrical drawing which would give information about the   4.____

    A. voltage drop in feeders
    B. size of feeders and panel loads
    C. external connections to equipment
    D. sequence of operation of devices and equipment

5. An electric motor driven air compressor is automatically started and stopped by a   5.____

    A. thermostat   B. line air valve
    C. pressure switch   D. float trap

6. The term *kilowatt hours* describes the consumption of   6.____

    A. energy   B. radiation
    C. cooling capacity   D. conductance

7. AC voltage may be converted to DC voltage by means of a   7.____

    A. magnet   B. rectifier
    C. voltage regulator   D. transducer

8. The metal which has the GREATEST resistance to the flow of electricity is   8.____

    A. steel   B. copper   C. silver   D. gold

9. Tinning a soldering iron means   9.____

    A. applying flux to the tip
    B. cleaning the tip to make it bright
    C. applying a coat of solder to the tip
    D. heating the iron to the proper temperature

10. Electricians working around *live wires* should wear gloves made of   10.____

    A. asbestos   B. metal mesh
    C. leather   D. rubber

11.   11.____

METER READING AT BEGENNING OF PERIOD

METER READING AT END OF PERIOD

The above are the readings on the electric meter at the beginning and end of a period. The TOTAL kilowatt hour consumption is

    A. 264   B. 570   C. 61   D. 175

12. The modern multiple-circuit program instrument which automatically controls bell signals in a school USUALLY includes   12.____

    A. automatic resetting of electric clocks throughout the school
    B. automatic ringing of room bells when the fire bell switch is closed
    C. prevention of manual control of schedules by eliminating manual control switches
    D. provision for automatic cutout of the schedule for any 24-hour day desired

13. Of the following, the device which uses the GREATEST amount of electric power is the   13.____

    A. electric typewriter
    B. $\frac{1}{4}$ inch electric drill
    C. floor scrubbing machine
    D. oil burner ignition transformer

14. Meters which indicate the electric power consumed in a public building are read in   14.____

    A. kilowatt-hours   B. volts
    C. cubic feet   D. degree days

15. The MAIN reason for grounding the outer shell of an electric fixture is to   15.____

    A. provide additional support for the fixture
    B. reduce the cost of installation of the fixture
    C. provide a terminal to which the wires can be attached
    D. reduce the chance of electric shock

16. The BEST way to determine whether the locknuts on terminals in an electrical terminal   16.____
box have become loose is to

    A. use an electric tester
    B. try to tighten the nuts with an appropriate wrench
    C. tap the nuts with an insulated handle
    D. try to loosen the nuts with a pair of pliers

17. The PROPER flux to use for soldering electric wire connections is   17.____

    A. rosin   B. killed acid
    C. borax   D. zinc chloride

18. A fusestat differs from an ordinary plug fuse in that a fusestat has   18.____

    A. less current carrying capacity
    B. different size threads
    C. an aluminum shell instead of a copper shell
    D. no threads

19. A grounding type 120-volt receptacle differs from an ordinary electric receptacle MAINLY   19.____
in that a grounding receptacle

    A. is larger than the ordinary receptacle
    B. has openings for a three prong plug
    C. can be used for larger machinery
    D. has a built-in circuit breaker

20. In a 110-220 volt three-wire circuit, the neutral wire is USUALLY   20.____

    A. black   B. red   C. white   D. green

21. Brushes on fractional horsepower universal motors are MOST often made of   21.____

    A. flexible copper strands   B. rigid carbon blocks
    C. thin wire strips   D. collector rings

22. A ground wire that is too small is dangerous because it will   22.____

    A. generate heat   B. blow a fuse
    C. increase the voltage   D. increase the current

23. A 115-volt hot water heater has a resistance of 5.75 ohms. The current it will take at   23.____
rated voltage is

    A. 15   B. 20   C. 13   D. 23

24. If a 30 ampere fuse is placed in a fuse box for a circuit requiring a 15 ampere fuse,   24.____

    A. serious damage to the circuit may result from an overload
    B. better protection will be provided for the circuit
    C. the larger fuse will tend to blow more often since it carries more current
    D. it will eliminate maintenance problems

25. Metal tubing through which electric wires of buildings are run is called   25.____

    A. insulation   B. conduit
    C. duct   D. sleeve

KEY (CORRECT ANSWERS)

1.	B	11.	D
2.	B	12.	A
3.	C	13.	C
4.	B	14.	A
5.	C	15.	D
6.	A	16.	B
7.	B	17.	A
8.	A	18.	B
9.	C	19.	B
10.	D	20.	C

21.	B
22.	A
23.	B
24.	A
25.	B

TEST 5

DIRECTIONS: Each question or incomplete statement is followed by several suggested answers or completions. Select the one that BEST answers the question or completes the statement. *PRINT THE LETTER OF THE CORRECT ANSWER IN THE SPACE AT THE RIGHT.*

1. *Found reading* and *left reading* are terms associated with   1.____

    A. petrometers   B. electric meters
    C. gas meters   D. water meters

2. When lamps are wired in parallel, the failure of one lamp will   2.____

    A. break the electric circuit to the other lamps
    B. have no effect on the power supply to the other lamps
    C. increase noticeably the light production of the other lamps
    D. cause excessive current to flow through the other lamps

3. The MAIN objection to using a copper penny in place of a blown fuse is that   3.____

    A. the penny will conduct electric current
    B. the penny will reduce the current flowing in the line
    C. melting of the penny will probably occur
    D. the line will not be protected against excessive current

4. The term *mogul base* is GENERALLY associated with   4.____

    A. boiler compound   B. stock cleaning solution
    C. insecticide   D. lamps

5. When connecting lamp sockets to a lighting circuit, the shell should ALWAYS be con-   5.____
nected to the white wire of the circuit to

    A. balance the load on the system
    B. reduce the possibility of accidental shock
    C. eliminate blowing the fuse in case the socket becomes grounded
    D. protect the circuit against reverse current

6. The MAIN purpose of periodic inspections and tests of electrical equipment is to   6.____

    A. encourage the workers to take better care of the equipment
    B. familiarize the workers with the equipment
    C. keep the workers busy during otherwise slack periods
    D. discover minor faults before they develop into major faults

7. The current rating of the fuse to use in a lighting circuit is determined by the   7.____

    A. connected load   B. line voltage
    C. capacity of the wiring   D. rating of the switch

8. Artificial respiration after a severe electric shock is ALWAYS necessary when the shock   8.____
results in

    A. unconsciousness   B. stoppage of breathing
    C. bleeding   D. a burn

9. If you find a co-worker lying unconscious across an electric wire, the FIRST thing you should do is   9._____

    A. get him off the wire   B. call the foreman
    C. get a doctor   D. shut off the power

10. A solenoid valve is actuated by   10._____

    A. air pressure   B. electric current
    C. temperature change   D. light rays

11.   11._____

The electrician's bit is indicated by the number

    A. 1   B. 2   C. 3   D. 4

12. BX is a designation for a type of   12._____

    A. flexible armored electric cable
    B. flexible gas line
    C. rigid conduit
    D. electrical insulation

13. *WYE-WYE* and *DELTA-WYE* are two   13._____

    A. types of DC motor windings
    B. arrangements of 3-phase transformer connections
    C. types of electrical splices
    D. shapes of commutator bars

14. When joining electric wires together in a fixture box, the BEST thing to use are wire   14._____

    A. connectors   B. couplings
    C. clamps   D. bolts

15. If the name plate of a motor indicates that it is a split phase motor, it is LIKELY that this motor   15.____

    A. is a universal motor
    B. operates on DC only
    C. operates on AC only
    D. operates either on DC at full power or on AC at reduced power

16. Rigid steel conduit used for the protection of electrical wiring is GENERALLY either galvanized or enameled both inside and out in order to   16.____

    A. prevent damage to the wire insulation
    B. make threading of the conduit easier
    C. prevent corrosion of the conduit
    D. make the conduit easier to handle

17. If a test lamp does not light when placed in series with a fuse and an appropriate battery, it is a GOOD indication that the fuse   17.____

    A. is open-circuited
    B. is short-circuited
    C. is in operating condition
    D. has zero resistance

18. The process of removing the insulation from a wire is called   18.____

    A. braiding   B. skinning   C. sweating   D. tinning

19. A 10-to-1 step-down transformer has an input of 1 ampere at 120 volts AC. If the losses are negligible, the output of the transformer is _____ volts.   19.____

    A. 1 ampere at 12   B. .1 ampere at 1200
    C. 10 amperes at 12   D. 10 amperes at 120

20. In city schools, wiring for motors or lighting is _____ volt, _____.   20.____

    A. 208-220; 4 wire, 60 cycle
    B. 240-110; 3 wire, 4 phase
    C. 120-208; 3 phase, 4 wire
    D. 160-210; 4 phase, 3 wire

21. When using a voltmeter in testing an electric circuit, the voltmeter should be connected   21.____

    A. across the circuit
    B. in series with the circuit
    C. in parallel or series with the circuit
    D. in series with the active element

22. A kilowatt is _____ watts.   22.____

    A. 500   B. 2,000   C. 1,500   D. 1,000

23. Of the following classifications, the one which pertains to fires in electrical equipment is Class   23.____

    A. A   B. B   C. C   D. D

24. The lighting systems in public buildings usually operate MOST NEARLY on _____ volts.   24._____

    A. 6   B. 24   C. 115   D. 220

25. A type of portable tool used to bend electrical conduit is called a   25._____

    A. helve   B. newel   C. spandrel   D. hickey

KEY (CORRECT ANSWERS)

1.	B		11.	C
2.	B		12.	A
3.	D		13.	B
4.	D		14.	A
5.	B		15.	C
6.	D		16.	C
7.	C		17.	A
8.	B		18.	B
9.	D		19.	C
10.	B		20.	B

21.	A
22.	D
23.	C
24.	C
25.	D

TEST 6

1. In a 4-wire, 3-phase electrical supply system, the voltage between one phase and ground used for the lighting load is MOST NEARLY

    A. 440   B. 230   C. 208   D. 115

1.____

2. Of the following, the one that takes the place of a fuse in an electrical circuit is a

    A. transformer   B. circuit breaker
    C. condenser   D. knife switch

2.____

3. Escutcheons are USUALLY located

    A. on switch plates
    B. on electrical outlets
    C. around pipes, to cover pipe sleeve openings
    D. around armored electric cable going into a gem box

3.____

4. It is ADVISABLE to remove broken bulbs from light sockets with

    A. a wooden or hard rubber wedge
    B. pliers
    C. a hammer and chisel
    D. a fuse puller

4.____

5. A 3-ohm resistor placed across a 12-volt battery will dissipate _____ watts.

    A. 3   B. 4   C. 12   D. 48

5.____

6. Instead of using fuses, modern electric wiring uses

    A. quick switches   B. circuit breakers
    C. fusible links   D. lag blocks

6.____

7. In order to reverse the direction of rotation of a series motor, the

    A. connections to the armature should be reversed
    B. connections to both the armature and the series field should be reversed
    C. connections of the motor to the power lines should be reversed
    D. series field should be placed in shunt with the armature

7.____

8. The BEST flux to use when soldering copper wires in an electric circuit is

    A. sal ammoniac   B. zinc chloride
    C. rosin   D. borax

8.____

9. A megger is an instrument used to measure

    A. capacitance   B. insulation resistance
    C. power   D. illumination levels

9.____

10. An electrical drawing is drawn to a scale of 1/4" = 1'.   10.____
If a length of conduit on the drawing measures 7 3/8", the actual length of the conduit,
in feet, is MOST NEARLY

    A. 7.5'   B. 15.5'   C. 22.5'   D. 29.5'

11. Standard 120-volt plug-type fuses are GENERALLY rated in   11.____

    A. farads   B. ohms   C. watts   D. amperes

12. Standard 120-volt electric light bulbs are GENERALLY rated in   12.____

    A. farads   B. ohms   C. watts   D. amperes

13. Of the following colors of electrical conductor coverings, the one which indicates a con-   13.____
ductor used SOLELY for grounding portable or fixed electrical equipment is

    A. blue   B. green   C. red   D. black

14. A device that operates to vary the resistance of an electrical circuit is USUALLY part of a   14.____
_____ pressuretrol.

    A. high-limit   B. low-limit
    C. manual-reset   D. modulating

15. The type of screwdriver SPECIALLY made to be used in tight spots is the   15.____

    A. Phillips   B. offset
    C. square shank   D. truss

16. On a plan, the symbol shown at the right USUALLY represents a(n)   16.____
    A. duplex receptacle
    B. electric switch
    C. ceiling outlet
    D. pull box

17. Electric power is measured in   17.____

    A. volts   B. amperes   C. watts   D. ohms

18. Of the following sizes of copper conductors, the one which has the LEAST current-carry-   18.____
ing capacity is _____ AWG.

    A. 000   B. 0   C. 8   D. 12

19. When excess current flows, a circuit breaker is opened directly by the action of a   19.____

    A. condenser   B. transistor
    C. relay   D. solenoid

20. Conduit is used in electrical wiring in order to the wires.   20.____

    A. waterproof   B. color code
    C. protect   D. insulate

KEY (CORRECT ANSWERS)

1.	D	11.	D
2.	B	12.	C
3.	D	13.	B
4.	A	14.	D
5.	B	15.	B
6.	B	16.	C
7.	A	17.	C
8.	C	18.	D
9.	B	19.	D
10.	D	20.	C

EXAMINATION SECTION
TEST 1

DIRECTIONS: Each question or incomplete statement is followed by several suggested answers or completions. Select the one that BEST answers the question or completes the statement. *PRINT THE LETTER OF THE CORRECT ANSWER IN THE SPACE AT THE RIGHT.*

1. Soft iron is MOST suitable for use in a   1.____
   A. permanent magnet   B. natural magnet
   C. temporary magnet   D. magneto

2. Static electricity is MOST often produced by   2.____
   A. pressure   B. magnetism   C. heat   D. friction

3. A fundamental law of electricity is that the current in a circuit is   3.____
   A. inversely proportional to the voltage
   B. equal to the voltage
   C. directly proportional to the resistance
   D. directly proportional to the voltage

4. A substance is classed as a magnet if it has   4.____
   A. the ability to conduct lines of force
   B. the property of high permeability
   C. the property of magnetism
   D. a high percentage of iron in its composition

5. If a compass is placed at the center of a bar magnet, the compass needle   5.____
   A. *points* to the geographic south pole
   B. *points* to the geographic north pole
   C. *alines* itself parallel to the bar
   D. *alines* itself perpendicular to the bar

6. When electricity is produced by heat in an iron-and-copper thermocouple, electrons   6.____
   move from
   A. north to south
   B. the hot junction, through the copper, across the cold junction to the iron, and then
      to the hot junction
   C. the hot junction, through the iron, across the cold junction to the copper, and then
      return through the copper to the hot junction
   D. east to west

7. The four factors affecting the resistance of a wire are its   7.____
   A. length, material, diameter, and temperature
   B. size, length, material, and insulation
   C. length, size, relative resistance, and material
   D. size, insulation, relative resistance, and material

8. Electricity in a battery is produced by   8.____

    A. chemical action
    B. chemical reaction
    C. a chemical acting upon metallic plates
    D. all of the above

9. Resistance is ALWAYS measured in   9.____

    A. coulombs   B. henrys   C. ohms   D. megohms

10. The magnetic pole that points northward on a compass   10.____

    A. is called the north pole
    B. is actually a south magnetic pole
    C. points to the north magnetic pole of the earth
    D. indicates the direction of the north geographic pole

11. Of the six methods of producing a voltage, which is the LEAST used?   11.____

    A. Chemical action   B. Heat
    C. Friction   D. Pressure

12. As the temperature of carbon is increased, its resistance will   12.____

    A. increase   B. decrease
    C. remain constant   D. double

13. Around a magnet, the external lines of force   13.____

    A. leave the magnet from the north pole and enter the south pole
    B. often cross one another
    C. leave the magnet from the south pole and enter the north pole
    D. may be broken by a piece of iron shielding

14. When a voltage is applied to a conductor, free electrons   14.____

    A. are forced into the nucleus of their atom
    B. are impelled along the conductor
    C. unite with protons
    D. cease their movement

15. When the molecules of a substance are altered, the action is referred to as   15.____

    A. thermal   B. photoelectric
    C. electrical   D. chemical

16. When matter is separated into individual atoms, it   16.____

    A. has undergone a physical change only
    B. has been reduced to its basic chemicals
    C. retains its original characteristics
    D. has been reduced to its basic elements

17. MOST permanent magnets and all electro-magnets are   17.____

    A. classed as natural magnets
    B. manufactured in various shapes from lodestone
    C. classed as artificial magnets
    D. manufactured in various shapes from magnetite

18. When a conductor moves across a magnetic field,   18.____

    A. a voltage is induced in the conductor
    B. a current is induced in the conductor
    C. both current and voltage are induced in the conductor
    D. neither a voltage nor a current is induced

19. The nucleus of an atom contains   19.____

    A. electrons and neutrons
    B. protons and neutrons
    C. protons and electrons
    D. protons, electrons, and neutrons

20. An alnico artificial magnet is composed of   20.____

    A. magnetite, steel, and nickel
    B. cobalt, nickel, and varnish
    C. aluminum, copper, and cobalt
    D. aluminum, nickel, and cobalt

21. A material that acts as an insulator for magnetic flux is   21.____

    A. glass   B. aluminum
    C. soft iron   D. unknown today

22. The force acting through the distance between two dissimilarly-charged bodies   22.____

    A. is a chemical force
    B. is referred to as a magnetic field
    C. constitutes a flow of ions
    D. is referred to as an electrostatic field

23. An atom that has lost or gained electrons   23.____

    A. is negatively charged   B. has a positive charge
    C. is said to be ionized   D. becomes electrically neutral

24. Which of the following is considered to be the BEST conductor?   24.____

    A. Zinc   B. Copper   C. Aluminum   D. Silver

25. As the temperature increases, the resistance of most conductors also increases.   25.____
     A conductor that is an EXCEPTION to this is

    A. aluminum   B. carbon   C. copper   D. brass

KEY (CORRECT ANSWERS)

1.	C		11.	C
2.	D		12.	B
3.	D		13.	A
4.	C		14.	B
5.	C		15.	D
6.	B		16.	D
7.	A		17.	C
8.	D		18.	A
9.	C		19.	B
10.	A		20.	D

21. D
22. D
23. C
24. D
25. B

TEST 2

DIRECTIONS: Each question or incomplete statement is followed by several suggested answers or completions. Select the one that BEST answers the question or completes the statement. *PRINT THE LETTER OF THE CORRECT ANSWER IN THE SPACE AT THE RIGHT.*

1. The dry cell battery is a _____ cell.   1._____

    A. secondary   B. polarized   C. primary   D. voltaic

2. The electrolyte of a lead-acid wet cell is   2._____

    A. sal ammoniac   B. manganese dioxide
    C. sulfuric acid   D. distilled water

3. A battery which can be restored after discharge is a _____ cell.   3._____

    A. primary   B. galvanic   C. dry   D. secondary

4. Lead-acid battery plates are held together by a   4._____

    A. glass wool mat   B. wood separator
    C. grid work   D. hard rubber tube

5. When mixing electrolyte, ALWAYS pour   5._____

    A. water into acid
    B. acid into water
    C. both acid and water into vat simultaneously
    D. first acid, then water into vat

6. When charging a battery, the electrolyte should NEVER exceed a temperature of   6._____

    A. 125° F.   B. 113° F.   C. 80° F.   D. 40° F.

7. The plates of a lead-acid battery are made of   7._____

    A. lead and lead dioxide   B. lead and lead oxide
    C. silver and peroxide   D. lead and lead peroxide

8. A battery is receiving a normal charge. It begins to gas freely.   8._____
   The charging current should

    A. be increased
    B. be decreased
    C. be cut off and the battery allowed to cool
    D. remain the same

9. A hydrometer reading is 1.265 at 92° F.   9._____
   The CORRECTED reading is

    A. 1.229   B. 1.261   C. 1.269   D. 1.301

10. In the nickel-cadmium battery, KOH is   10._____

    A. the positive plate   B. the negative plate
    C. the electrolyte   D. none of the above

11. When sulfuric acid, H_2SO_4, and water, H_2O, are mixed together, they form a   11.____

    A. gas   B. compound
    C. mixture   D. hydrogen solution

12. How many No. 6 dry cells are required to supply power to a load requiring 6 volts if the   12.____
cells are connected in series?

    A. Two   B. Four   C. Five   D. Six

13. The ordinary 6-volt lead-acid storage battery consists of how many cells?   13.____

    A. Two   B. Three   C. Four   D. Six

14. A fully-charged aircraft battery has a specific gravity reading of   14.____

    A. 1.210 to 1.220   B. 1.250 to 1.265
    C. 1.285 to 1.300   D. 1.300 to 1.320

15. What is the ampere-hour rating of a storage battery that can deliver 20 amperes continu-   15.____
ously for 10 hours?
_____ ampere-hour.

    A. 20   B. 40   C. 200   D. 400

16. The normal cell voltage of a fully-charged nickel-cadmium battery is _____ volts.   16.____

    A. 2.0   B. 1.5   C. 1.4   D. 1.0

17. The electrolyte in a mercury cell is   17.____

    A. sulfuric acid
    B. KOH
    C. potassium hydroxide, zincate, and mercury
    D. potassium hydroxide, water, and zincate

18. Concentrated sulfuric acid has a specific gravity of   18.____

    A. 1.285   B. 1.300   C. 1.830   D. 2.400

19. The number of negative plates in a lead-acid cell is ALWAYS _____ of positive plates.   19.____

    A. one greater than the number
    B. equal to the number
    C. one less than the number
    D. double the number

20. A lead-acid battery is considered fully charged when the specific gravity readings of all   20.____
cells taken at half-hour intervals show no change for _____ hour(s).

    A. four   B. three   C. two   D. one

KEY (CORRECT ANSWERS)

1.	C	11.	C
2.	C	12.	B
3.	D	13.	B
4.	C	14.	C
5.	B	15.	C
6.	A	16.	C
7.	D	17.	D
8.	B	18.	C
9.	C	19.	A
10.	C	20.	A

———

TEST 3

DIRECTIONS: Each question or incomplete statement is followed by several suggested answers or completions. Select the one that BEST answers the question or completes the statement. *PRINT THE LETTER OF THE CORRECT ANSWER IN THE SPACE AT THE RIGHT.*

1. In which direction does current flow in an electrical circuit?   1.____

   A. - to + externally, + to - internally
   B. + to - externally, + to - internally
   C. - to + externally, - to + internally
   D. + to - externally, - to + internally

2. Given the formula $P = E^2/R$, solve for E.   2.____

   A. $E = \sqrt{ER}$ B. $E = \sqrt{PR}$ C. $E = IR$ D. $E = \sqrt{P/R}$

3. Resistance in the power formula equals   3.____

   A. $R = \sqrt{I/P}$ B. $R = E/I$ C. $R = \sqrt{P \times 1}$ D. $R = E^2/P$

4. One joule is equal to   4.____

   A. 1 watt second   B. 10 watt seconds
   C. 1 watt minute   D. 10 watt minutes

5. A lamp has a source voltage of 110 v. and a current of 0.9 amps.   5.____
   What is the resistance of the lamp?

   A. 12.22 Ω   B. 122.2 Ω   C. 0.008 Ω   D. 0.08 Ω

6. In accordance with Ohm's law, the relationship between current and voltage in a simple   6.____
   circuit is that the

   A. current varies inversely with the resistance if the voltage is held constant
   B. voltage varies as the square of the applied e.m.f.
   C. current varies directly with the applied voltage if the resistance is held constant
   D. voltage varies inversely as the current if the resistance is held constant

7. The current needed to operate a soldering iron which has a rating of 600 watts at 110   7.____
   volts is

   A. 0.182 a.   B. 5.455 a.   C. 18.200 a.   D. 66.000 a.

8. In electrical circuits, the time rate of doing work is expressed in   8.____

   A. volts   B. amperes   C. watts   D. ohms

9. If the resistance is held constant, what is the relationship between power and voltage in a   9.____
   simple circuit?

   A. Resistance must be varied to show a true relationship.
   B. Power will vary as the square of the applied voltage.
   C. Voltage will vary inversely proportional to power.
   D. Power will vary directly with voltage.

10. How many watts are there in 1 horsepower?   10.____

    A. 500   B. 640   C. 746   D. 1,000

11. What formula is used to find watt-hours?   11.____

    A. $E \times T$ B. $E \times I \times T$ C. $E \times I \times \sqrt{\theta}$ D. $E \times I^2$

12. What is the resistance of the circuit shown at the right?   12.____

    A. $4.8\,\Omega$

    B. $12.0\,\Omega$

    C. $48\,\Omega$

    D. $120\,\Omega$

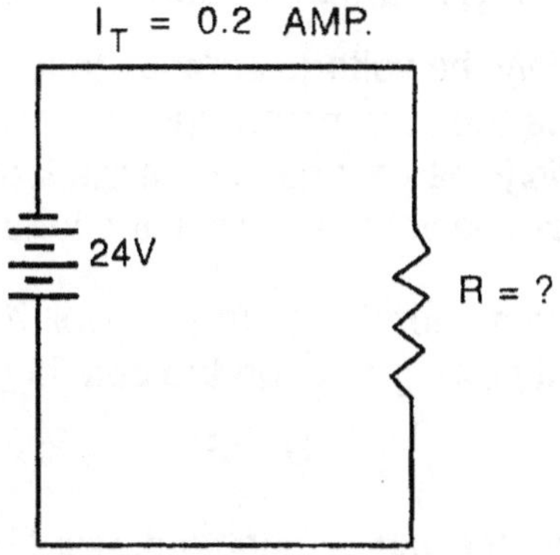

$I_T = 0.2$ AMP.

24V

$R = ?$

13. In the figure at the right, solve for I_T.   13.____

    A. 0.5 a.

    B. 1 a.

    C. 13 a.

    D. 169 a.

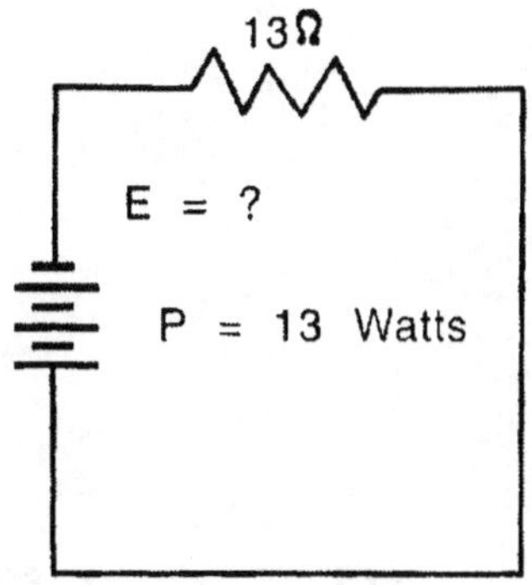

$13\,\Omega$

$E = ?$

$P = 13$ Watts

14. A simple circuit consists of one power source,   14.____

    A. and one power consuming device

    B. one power consuming device, and connecting wiring

    C. protective device, and control device

    D. one power consuming device, and protective device

15. The device used in circuits to prevent damage from overloads is called a   15.____

    A. fuse   B. switch   C. resistor   D. connector

16. What happens in a series circuit when the voltage remains constant and the resistance increases?   16.____

Current

    A. increases   B. decreases

    C. remains the same   D. increases by the square

17. Other factors remaining constant, what would be the effect on the current flow in a given circuit if the applied potential were doubled?
It would

   A. double   B. remain the same
   C. be divided by two   D. be divided by four

18. Which of the following procedures can be used to calculate the resistance of a load?

   A. *Multiply* the voltage across the load by the square of the current through the load
   B. *Divide* the current through the load by the voltage across the load
   C. *Multiply* the voltage across the load by the current through the load
   D. *Divide* the voltage across the load by the current through the load

19. A cockpit light operates from a 24-volt d-c supply and uses 72 watts of power. The current flowing through the bulb is _____ amps.

   A. 0.33   B. 3   C. 600   D. 1,728

20. If the resistance is held constant, what happens to power if the current is doubled?
Power is

   A. doubled   B. multiplied by 4
   C. halved   D. divided by 4

KEY (CORRECT ANSWERS)

1. A		11. B
2. B		12. D
3. D		13. B
4. A		14. B
5. B		15. A
6. C		16. B
7. B		17. A
8. C		18. D
9. B		19. B
10. C		20. B

TEST 4

DIRECTIONS: Each question or incomplete statement is followed by several suggested answers or completions. Select the one that BEST answers the question or completes the statement. *PRINT THE LETTER OF THE CORRECT ANSWER IN THE SPACE AT THE RIGHT.*

1. If a circuit is constructed so as to allow the electrons to follow only one possible path, the circuit is called a(n) _____ circuit.   1._____

    A. series-parallel   B. incomplete
    C. series   D. parallel

2. According to Kirchhoff's Law of Voltages, the algebraic sum of all the voltages in a series circuit is equal to   2._____

    A. zero
    B. source voltage
    C. total voltage drop
    D. the sum of the IR drop of the circuit

3. In a series circuit, the total current is   3._____

    A. always equal to the source voltage
    B. determined by the load only
    C. the same through all parts of the circuit
    D. equal to zero at the positive side of the source

4.   4._____

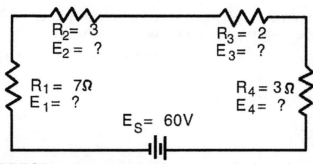

The CORRECT voltage equation for the circuit above is

    A. $E_S + E_1 + E_2 + E_3 + E_4 = 0$
    B. $E_S - E_1 - E_2 - E_3 - E_4 = 0$
    C. $E_S = -E_1 - E_2 - E_3 - E_4$
    D. $-E_S = E_1 + E_2 + E_3 + E_4$

5. Referring to the circuit shown in Question 4 above, after expressing the voltage drops around the circuit in terms of current and resistance and the given values of source voltage, the equation becomes   5._____

    A. $-60 - 71 - 31 - 21 - 31 = 0$
    B. $-60 + 71 + 31 + 21 + 31 = 0$
    C. $60 - 71 - 31 - 21 - 31 = 0$
    D. $60 + 71 + 31 + 21 + 31 = 0$

6. By the use of the correct equation, it is found that the current (I) in the circuit shown in Question 4 is of positive value. This indicates that the

6.____

    A. assumed direction of current flow is correct
    B. assumed direction of current flow is incorrect
    C. problem is not solvable
    D. battery polarity should be reversed

7.

7.____

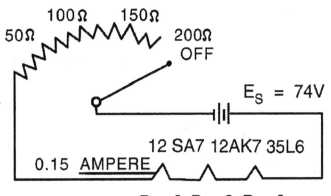

$$R_1 = ? \quad R_2 = ? \quad R_3 = ?$$

In what position would the variable rheostat in the circuit above be placed in order that the filaments of the tubes operate properly with a current flow of 0.15 ampere? _____ position.

    A. 50 Ω B. 100Ω C. 150 Ω D. 200Ω

8. The power absorbed by the variable rheostat in the circuit used in Question 7 above, when placed in its proper operating position, would be _____ watts.

8.____

    A. 112.50   B. 2.25   C. 337.50   D. 450.00

9.

9.____

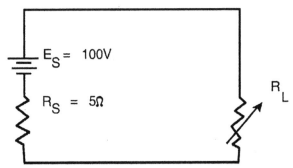

In the circuit above, maximum power would be transferred from the source to the load (R_L) if R_L were set at _____ ohms.

    A. 2   B. 5   C. 12   D. 24

10.

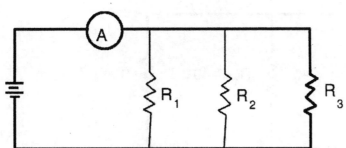

In the circuit above, if an additional resistor were placed in parallel to R_3, the ammeter reading would

A. increase
C. remain the same

B. decrease
D. drop to zero

11. In a parallel circuit containing a 4-ohm, 5-ohm, and 6-ohm resistor, the current flow is

A. *highest* through the 4-ohm resistor
B. *lowest* through the 4-ohm resistor
C. *highest* through the 6-ohm resistor
D. *equal* through all three resistors

12. Three resistors of 2, 4, and 6 ohms, respectively, are connected in parallel. Which resistor would absorb the GREATEST power?

A. The 2-ohm resistor
B. The 4-ohm resistor
C. The 6-ohm resistor
D. It will be the same for all resistors

13. If three lamps are connected in parallel with a power source, connecting a fourth lamp in parallel will

A. *decrease* E_T
C. *increase* E_T

B. *decrease* I_T
D. *increase* I_T

14.

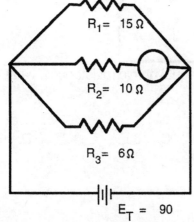

What is the current flow through the ammeter in the circuit shown above?
_____ amps.

A. 4   B. 9   C. 15   D. 28

15.   15.____

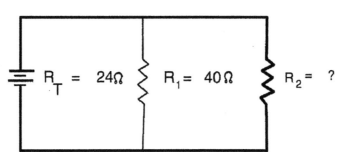

In the circuit shown above, the TOTAL resistance is 24 ohms. What is the value of R_2?
_____ ohms.

   A. 16   B. 40   C. 60   D. 64

16.   16.____

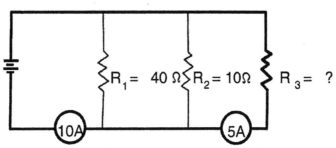

What is the source voltage of the circuit shown above?
_____ volts.

   A. 40   B. 50   C. 100   D. 500

17. What is the value of R_3 in the circuit shown in Question 16 above?   17.____
      _____ ohms.

   A. 8   B. 10   C. 20   D. 100

18.   18.____

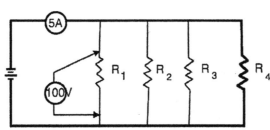

If all 4 resistors in the circuit above are of equal ohmic resistances, what is the value of R_3?
_____ ohms.

   A. 5   B. 20   C. 60   D. 80

19.

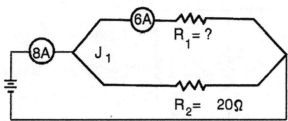

What is the value of the source voltage in the circuit above?

_____ volts

A. 20   B. 40   C. 120   D. 160

20.

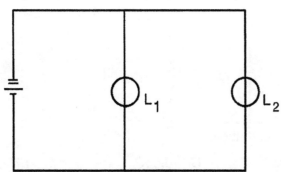

If Lamp L_2 in the circuit above should suddenly burn out, which of the statements below is CORRECT?

A. More current would flow through lamp L_1.
B. Source voltage would decrease.
C. The filament resistance of lamp L_1 would decrease.
D. Lamp L_1 would still burn normal.

21. When referring to a circuit's conductance, you visualize the degree to which the circuit

A. *permits* or conducts voltage
B. *opposes* the rate of voltage changes
C. *permits* or conducts current flow
D. *opposes* the rate of current flow

22.

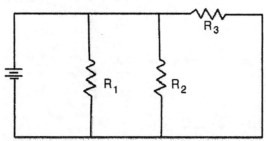

The TOTAL conductance of the circuit above would be solved by which of the equations?

A. $G_T - G_1 - G_2 - G_3 = 0$
C. $G_T = G_1 - G_2 - G_3$

B. $G_T + G_1 + G_2 + G_3 = 0$
D. $G_T = G_1 + G_2 + G_3$

23.

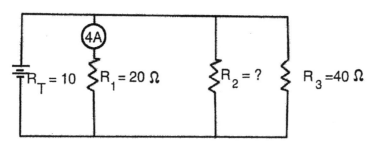

23.____

If the resistors in the circuit above are all rated at 250 watts, which resistor or resistors would overheat?

A. R_1 B. R_2 C. R_3 D. All

24.

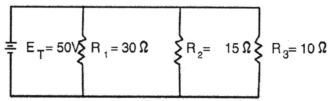

24.____

The TOTAL conductance of the circuit above is

A. 0.15G   B. 0.20G   C. 0.50G   D. 0.75G

KEY (CORRECT ANSWERS)

1. C		11. A	
2. A		12. A	
3. C		13. D	
4. B		14. B	
5. C		15. C	
6. A		16. A	
7. B		17. A	
8. B		18. D	
9. B		19. B	
10. A		20. D	

21. C
22. D
23. A
24. B

TEST 5

DIRECTIONS: Each question or incomplete statement is followed by several suggested answers or completions. Select the one that BEST answers the question or completes the statement. *PRINT THE LETTER OF THE CORRECT ANSWER IN THE SPACE AT THE RIGHT.*

1. The MINIMUM number of resistors in a compound circuit is (are)   1.____

    A. four   B. three   C. two   D. one

2.   2.____

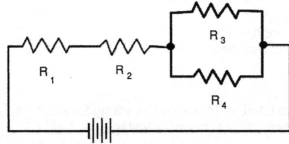

Total resistance of the circuit shown is determined by the formula

    A. $R_1 R_2 + \dfrac{R_3 R_4}{R_4 + R_3}$ B. $R_1 + R_2 + \dfrac{R_3 + R_4}{R_3 R_4}$

    C. $R_1 + R_2 + \dfrac{R_3 R_4}{R_3 + R_4}$ D. $R_1 + R_2 + (\dfrac{R_3 R_4}{R_3 + R_4})$

3.   3.____

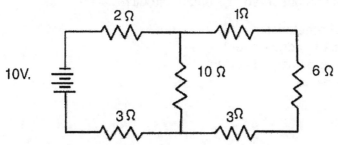

In the circuit above, what is the value of I_t?

$I_t =$ _____ amp.

    A. 1.14   B. 0.4   C. 0.667   D. 1

4. In the circuit in Question 3 above, how much power is consumed by the 6-ohm resistor?   4.____
_____ watts.

    A. 15   B. 1.5   C. 60   D. 6

5. A voltage divider is used to   5.____

    A. provide different voltage values for multiple loads from a single source
    B. provide several voltage drops in parallel
    C. increase the voltage to the load at several taps
    D. provide tap points to alter power supplied

6. The total power supplied to the entire circuit by a voltage divider and 4 loads is the   6.____

    A. sum of the 4 loads
    B. voltage divider minus 4 loads
    C. voltage divider plus the 4 loads
    D. voltage divider only

7. The total voltage of a voltage divider is the   7.____

    A. input voltage minus the load's voltages
    B. the load's voltages only
    C. sum of the input and load voltage
    D. sum of the voltages across the divider

8. An attenuator is   8.____

    A. a network of resistors used to reduce power, voltage, or current
    B. a network of resistors to change the input voltage
    C. also called a pad
    D. used in every power circuit

9. In an attenuator, the resistors are   9.____

    A. adjusted separately
    B. connected in parallel with the load
    C. connected in series with the load
    D. ganged

10. What two conditions may be observed in a bridge circuit?   10.____

    A. T and L network characteristics
    B. No-load and full-load bridge current
    C. Unequal potential and unequal current
    D. Balance and unbalance

11.   11.____

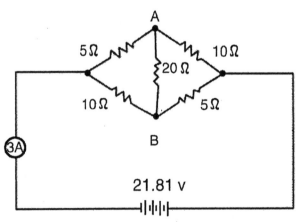

In the circuit above, how much current flows in the resistor and what is its direction?

    A. 26 a.; B to A   B. la.; A to B
    C. 0.273 a.; A to B   D. la.; B to A

12. In a three-wire distribution system, an unbalanced situation is indicated by the   12.____

    A. potential of the positive wire being equal to the negative wire
    B. positive wire carrying more amperage than the negative wire
    C. current in the neutral wire
    D. neutral wire carrying the total current

13.   13.____

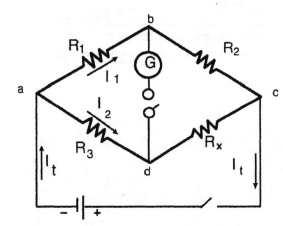

SCHEMATIC
WHEATSTONE-BRIDGE
CIRCUIT

In the figure above, the galvanometer will show zero deflection when

A. $\dfrac{R_1}{R_2} + \dfrac{R_3}{R_x}$

B. $R_x = \dfrac{R_1 R_3}{R_2}$

C. $\dfrac{I_1 R_1}{I_2 R_x} = \dfrac{I_2 R_3}{I_1 R_2}$

D. $R_x = \dfrac{R_1 R_2}{R_3}$

14. In the Wheatstone Bridge type circuit shown at the right, the bridge current is toward Point A.
The resistance of R_x is   14.____

    A. $30\,\Omega$
    B. greater than $45\,\Omega$
    C. $20\,\Omega$
    D. less than $15\,\Omega$

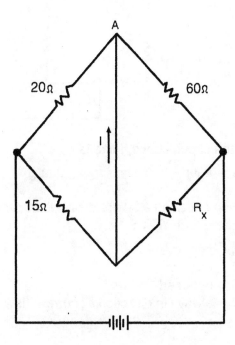

15.   15.____

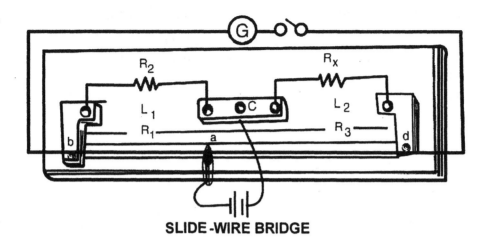

SLIDE-WIRE BRIDGE

In the slide-wire bridge shown above, L_1 is equal to

A. $L_1 = \dfrac{R_2 L_2}{R_1}$ B. $L_1 = \dfrac{R_1 + L_2}{R_2}$

C. $\dfrac{R_2}{R_1 L_2} = L_1$ D. $\dfrac{R_2 L_2}{R_x} = L_1$

16.   16.____

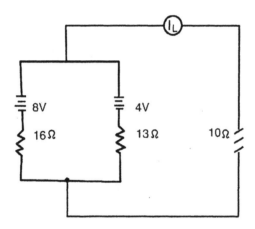

In the circuit above, I line is

A.   4.44 a.   B.   0.444 a.   C.   0.337 a.   D.   5.22 a.

17.   When checking a 3-wire distribution circuit going against the direction of current flow, the   17.____
      IR drop is ALWAYS

      A.   negative
      B.   positive
      C.   not used
      D.   always in direction of current flow

18.

In the circuit above, the voltage drop across the 3-ohm resistor is _____ volts.

A. 2.4   B. 24   C. 9.6   D. 0.96

18.____

19. The resistance of the wire is taken into consideration in the 2- and 3-wire distribution systems because the

   A. source and load are very close
   B. resistance of the wire is the same throughout
   C. load and source are at a considerable distance from each other
   D. load must be decreased in order to determine accurate circuit values

19.____

20. What is Kirchhoff's second law as applied to 3-wire distribution circuits?

   A. Sum of all the voltages is zero.
   B. Algebraic sum of all the voltages about closed path is zero.
   C. Algebraic sum of all voltage is zero.
   D. All IR drops in the circuit are negative.

20.____

———

KEY (CORRECT ANSWERS)

1.	B	11.	C
2.	C	12.	C
3.	D	13.	A
4.	B	14.	B
5.	A	15.	D
6.	C	16.	C
7.	D	17.	B
8.	A	18.	A
9.	D	19.	C
10.	D	20.	B

———

TEST 6

DIRECTIONS: Each question or incomplete statement is followed by several suggested answers or completions. Select the one that BEST answers the question or completes the statement. *PRINT THE LETTER OF THE CORRECT ANSWER IN THE SPACE AT THE RIGHT.*

1. A mil is what part of an inch?   1._____

    A. 1/10   B. 1/100
    C. 1/1000   D. 1/1,000,000

2. The discharge (electrical leakage) that MIGHT occur from a wire carrying a high potential   2._____
   is called

    A. arcing   B. sparking
    C. static discharge   D. corona

3. Bare wire ends are spliced by the   3._____

    A. western union method   B. rat-tail joint method
    C. fixture joint method   D. all of the above

4. What is a unit conductor called that has a length of one foot and a cross-sectional area of   4._____
   one circular mil?

    A. Square mil   B. Circular mil
    C. Circular mil foot   D. Square mil foot

5. The induction-type soldering iron is commonly known as the   5._____

    A. soldering copper   B. pencil iron
    C. soldering gun   D. resistance gun

6. All good quality soldering irons operate at what temperature?   6._____

    A. 400 - 500° F.   B. 500 - 600° F.
    C. 600 - 700° F.   D. 300 - 600° F.

7. A No. 12 wire has a diameter of 80.81 mils.   7._____
   What is the area in circular mils?
   _____ cm.

    A. 6,530   B. 5,630   C. 4,530   D. 3,560

8. Dielectric strength is the   8._____

    A. opposite of potential difference
    B. ability of a conductor to carry large amounts of current
    C. ability of an insulator to withstand a potential difference
    D. strength of a magnetic field

9. To readily transfer the heat from the soldering iron tip, it FIRST should be   9._____

    A. tinned with solder
    B. allowed to form an oxide film
    C. cleaned with carbon tetrachloride
    D. allowed to heat for 25 minutes

10. A No. 12 wire has a diameter of 80.81 mils.
What is the area in square mils?
_____ square mils.

    A. 2,516.8   B. 5,128.6   C. 6,530   D. 8,512.6

10.____

11. Varnished cambric insulation is used to cover conductors carrying voltages above
_____ volts.

    A. 1,000   B. 1,500   C. 15,000   D. 5,000

11.____

12. The solder splicer is used to

    A. prevent the waste of rosin core solder
    B. connect together small lengths of solder
    C. connect two conductors together
    D. none of the above

12.____

13. The conductance of a conductor is the ease with which current will flow through it.
It is measured in

    A. ohms   B. mhos   C. henrys   D. amperes

13.____

14. Asbestos insulation loses its insulating properties when it becomes

    A. overaged
    B. overheated
    C. used over a long period of time
    D. wet

14.____

15. How are solderless connectors installed on conductors?

    A. Bolted on   B. Chemical compound
    C. Crimped on   D. All of the above

15.____

16. The factor(s) governing the selection of wire size is (are)

    A. (I^2R loss) in the line
    B. (IR drop) in the line
    C. current-carrying ability of the line
    D. all of the above

16.____

17. Enamel insulated conductors are USUALLY called

    A. magnet wire   B. high voltage wire
    C. low voltage wire   D. transmission lines

17.____

18. The advantage of solderless connectors over soldered-type connectors is that they are

    A. mechanically stronger   B. easier to install
    C. free of corrosion   D. all of the above

18.____

19. The basic requirement of any splice is that it be   19._____

    A. soldered
    B. mechanically and electrically as strong as the conductor that is spliced
    C. made with a splicer
    D. taped

20. The type of tape that is used for electrical circuits having a temperature of 175° F. or   20._____
above is

    A. glass cloth
    B. plastic
    C. synthetic rubber compound
    D. impregnated cloth

KEY (CORRECT ANSWERS)

1.	C	11.	C
2.	D	12.	C
3.	D	13.	B
4.	C	14.	D
5.	A	15.	C
6.	B	16.	D
7.	A	17.	A
8.	C	18.	B
9.	A	19.	B
10.	B	20.	A

EXAMINATION SECTION
TEST 1

DIRECTIONS: Each question or incomplete statement is followed by several suggested
answers or completions. Select the one that *BEST* answers the question or
completes the statement. *PRINT THE LETTER OF THE CORRECT ANSWER
IN THE SPACE AT THE RIGHT.*

1. Asbestos was used as a wire covering mainly for protection against   1._____

    A.   humidity   B.   vibration   C.   corrosion   D.   heat

2. A wattmeter is used for making a direct measurement of   2._____

    A.   current   B.   voltage   C.   power   D.   resistance

3. The number of connection points to a two-pole, double-throw knife switch is   3._____

    A.   2   B.   4   C.   6   D.   8

4. Wires are pulled through conduit with the aid of   4._____

    A.   a hickey   B.   an extension bit
    C.   a snake   D.   a nipple

5. To smooth out the ripples present in rectified a.c., the device commonly used is a   5._____

    A.   filter   B.   relay   C.   spark gap   D.   booster

6. A tachometer is used for measuring   6._____

    A.   r.p.m.   B.   torque
    C.   power factor   D.   specific gravity

7. Rubber insulation deteriorates most rapidly when in contact with   7._____

    A.   water   B.   oil   C.   lead   D.   aluminum

8. The microfarad is a unit of measurement used for condenser   8._____

    A.   ohmic resistance   B.   power loss
    C.   leakage current   D.   capacity

9. A "megger" is an electrical instrument used to measure   9._____

    A.   current   B.   resistance
    C.   voltage   D.   wattage

10. When a run of conduit would require many right angle bends, it is necessary to install pull   10._____
boxes because

    A.   conduit cannot be bent
    B.   otherwise injury to the wires may result during installation
    C.   conduit comes in fixed lengths
    D.   the conduit requires support

11. The metal frames of some electrical units are grounded mainly to   11.____

    A. eliminate short-circuits
    B. save insulating material
    C. protect against shock
    D. prevent overloading

12. A motor which can be operated only from an a.c. power source is   12.____

    A. a shunt motor   B. a series motor
    C. a compound motor   D. an induction motor

13. Of the following, the poorest conductor of electricity is   13.____

    A. mercury   B. sulphuric acid
    C. distilled water   D. salt water

14. The insulation provided between commutator bars on a d.c. motor is generally   14.____

    A. mica   B. lucite   C. porcelain   D. transite

15. Nichrome wire should be most suitable for use in   15.____

    A. a transformer   B. a motor
    C. an incandescent lamp   D. a heating element

16. Electrical outlet boxes do not have to be drilled for the entrance of conduit into the boxes   16.____
if they are provided with

    A. bushings   B. knockouts   C. hickeys   D. couplings

17. The minimum number of field windings in a compound motor is   17.____

    A. 1   B. 2   C. 3   D. 4

18. The motor most likely to reach a dangerous speed if operated at normal voltage and no   18.____
load is a

    A. shunt motor   B. series motor
    C. compound motor   D. synchronous motor

19. If three 6-volt batteries are connected in parallel, the resultant voltage will be   19.____

    A. 18 volts   B. 9 volts   C. 6 volts   D. 2 volts

20. If an incandescent lamp is operated at a voltage below its rated voltage then it   20.____

    A. will operate more efficiently
    B. will have a longer life
    C. will take more power
    D. is more likely to fail by arcing

21. Four resistors, having respective current ratings of 1, 2, 3 and 4 amperes, are connected   21.____
in series. If the resistors are not to be overloaded, the maximum current permissable in
this circuit is

    A. 1ampere   B. 2.5 amperes
    C. 4 amperes   D. 10 amperes

22. Conduit is reamed mainly to

    A. protect the wires against sharp edges
    B. make threading easier
    C. increase its electrical conductivity
    D. improve its appearance

22.____

23. Two 25-watt, 120-volt lamps are connected in parallel to a 120-volt source. The two lamps will take a total of

    A. 12.5 watts   B. 25 watts
    C. 50 watts   D. 100 watts

23.____

24. An advantage of the mercury arc rectifiers when compared to rotary converters is that the mercury arc rectifiers

    A. are relatively quiet
    B. eliminate the use of transformers
    C. operate at lower voltage
    D. operate for shorter periods

24.____

25. A bushing is usually provided on the end of a conduit running into a panel box. An important function of the bushing is to

    A. insulate the conduit from the panel box
    B. support the panel box
    C. separate one conduit from another
    D. prevent injury to the wires

25.____

26. An alternator is

    A. an a.c. generator
    B. a ground detector device
    C. a choke coil
    D. a frequency meter

26.____

27. The best immediate first-aid treatment for a scraped knee is to

    A. apply plain vaseline
    B. use a knee splint
    C. apply heat
    D. wash it with soap and water

27.____

Questions 28 - 34.

Questions 28 through 34 are based on the Signal System Emergency Power Supply Information given below. Read this information carefully before answering these questions.

SIGNAL SYSTEM EMERGENCY POWER SUPPLY INFORMATION

The signal mains operate on 115 volts a.c. and are fed from either a normal power supply or an emergency power supply. When the normal power supply goes below 90 volts, a transfer switch automatically switches the signal mains to the emergency power. With normal feed, the transfer switch is held in the normal or energized position. When the normal power supply falls, the transfer switch changes to the emergency supply by means of gravity and a control spring. The operation of the transfer switch is controlled by means of a potential relay which opens on less than 90 volts. Once the transfer switch has changed to the emergency side, it can only be reset to the normal side by first closing the potential relay by hand. If the normal supply is satisfactory, this relay will remain closed. Then by pushing a reset button, the transfer switch will swing to the normal side and remain-closed through its retaining circuit. A special push button is provided for checking the transfer switch for proper operation.

28. The transfer switch will automatically connect the signal mains to emergency power when the normal power supply voltage is

    A. 120 volts   B. 115 volts   C. 95 volts   D. 85 volts

28._____

29. The *FIRST* step in resetting the transfer switch to the normal side is to

    A. open the potential relay   B. push the reset button
    C. operate the special button   D. close the potential relay

29._____

30. The special push button is provided for

    A. checking the operation of the transfer switch
    B. disconnecting the emergency supply
    C. automatically closing the potential relay
    D. resetting the control spring

30._____

31. The reset button is used to

    A. swing the transfer switch to the normal side
    B. swing the transfer switch to the emergency side
    C. energize the potential relay
    D. de-energize the potential relay

31._____

32. The signal mains receive their power through the

    A. potential relay   B. transfer switch
    C. reset button   D. special push button

32._____

33. When the emergency power is feeding the signal mains, then the

    A. transfer switch is automatically energized
    B. potential relay automatically goes to the closed position
    C. transfer switch is in the de-energized position
    D. special push button must be pressed to restore the normal power supply

33._____

34. The transfer switch is held in the emergency supply position by

    A. a retaining circuit
    B. a special push button
    C. gravity and a control spring
    D. a reset button

34._____

35. To reduce the pitting of relay contacts which make and break frequently, the unit generally connected across them is a

    A. transistor   B. spark gap
    C. condenser   D. switch

35._____

36. As compared to a solid conductor, a stranded conductor of the same diameter 36.____

    A. has greater flexibility
    B. requires less insulation
    C. has greater resistance to corrosion
    D. does not require soldered connections

37. The electrolyte in a lead storage battery is 37.____

    A. sodium bicarbonate   B. sulphuric acid
    C. muriatic acid   D. ammonia

38. Twisted pair wire is desirable for telephone circuits mainly because it 38.____

    A. is less likely to pick up electrical interference
    B. can be run in long stretches without any support
    C. can carry heavy currents
    D. can withstand high voltage

39. In the subway, heavy copper bonds are connected across the joints of the track rails. With the bonds installed, a voltage drop measurement is taken across the track rail joint. This test would be used mainly to determine the bond 39.____

    A. temperature   B. electrical resistance
    C. breakdown voltage   D. leakage current

40. In a polarized electric cord plug, the contact blades of the plug are 40.____

    A. magnetized
    B. of different color
    C. parallel to each other
    D. perpendicular to each other

41. A capacity rating expressed in ampere-hours is commonly used for 41.____

    A. insulators   B. storage batteries
    C. switches   D. inductances

42. The number of ordinary flashlight cells which must be connected together to obtain 6 volts is 42.____

    A. 1   B. 2   C. 3   D. 4

43. A bank of five 120-volt lamps connected in series is used for test purposes in the subway. This test bank would be best utilized in checking a circuit having 43.____

    A. 120 volts d.c.   B. 120 volts a.c.
    C. 24 volts   D. 600 volts

44. A step-up transformer is used to step up 44.____

    A. voltage   B. current   C. power   D. frequency

45. A photoelectric cell is a device for changing   45.____

    A. light into electricity
    B. electricity into light
    C. electricity into heat
    D. sound into electricity

46. Decreasing the length of a wire conductor will   46.____

    A. increase the current carrying capacity
    B. decrease the current carrying capacity
    C. decrease the resistance
    D. increase the resistance

47. The proper tool to use in making a hole through a transite panel is   47.____

    A. a star drill   B. a countersink
    C. a twist drill   D. an auger

48. Copper is a preferred metal in the construction of large knife switches because it is   48.____

    A. soft   B. flexible
    C. a good conductor   D. light in weight

49. The process of removing the insulation from a wire is called   49.____

    A. sweating   B. skinning
    C. tinning   D. braiding

50. The electric lamp which is used for providing heat is   50.____

    A. a sodium vapor lamp   B. a mercury vapor lamp
    C. a neon lamp   D. an infra-red lamp

KEY (CORRECT ANSWERS)

1. D	11. C	21. A	31. A	41. B
2. C	12. D	22. A	32. B	42. D
3. C	13. C	23. C	33. C	43. D
4. C	14. A	24. A	34. C	44. A
5. A	15. D	25. D	35. C	45. A
6. A	16. B	26. A	36. A	46. C
7. B	17. B	27. D	37. B	47. C
8. D	18. B	28. D	38. A	48. C
9. B	19. C	29. D	39. B	49. B
10. B	20. B	30. A	40. D	50. D

TEST 2

DIRECTIONS: Each question or incomplete statement is followed by several suggested answers or completions. Select the one that *BEST* answers the question or completes the statement. *PRINT THE LETTER OF THE CORRECT ANSWER IN THE SPACE AT THE RIGHT.*

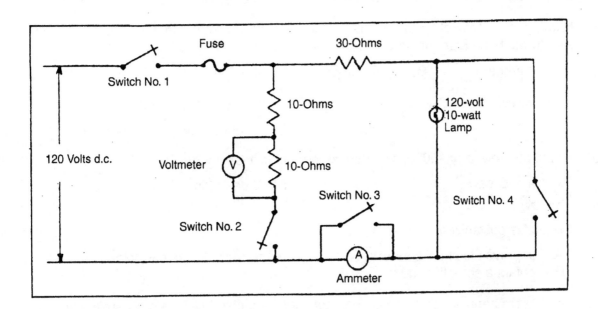

Questions 1-7

Questions 1 through 7 are based on the above wiring diagram. Refer to this diagram when answering these questions.

1. Starting with all switches open, then to light the lamp it is necessary to close switch   1.____

    A. No. 1   B. No. 2   C. No. 3   D. No . 4

2. Closing one of the four switches will prevent the lamp from being lighted. This switch is   2.____

    A. No. 1   B. No. 2   C. No. 3   D. No. 4

3. The two switches which must be in the closed position to obtain a reading on the voltme-   3.____
    ter are

    A. No. 1 and No. 4   B. No. 2 and No. 3
    C. No. 3 and No. 4   D. No.1 and No. 2

4. To obtain a reading on the ammeter it is necessary to have   4.____

    A. switch No. 2 open
    B. switch No. 4 closed
    C. switch No. 3 closed and switch No. 1 open
    D. switch No. 3 open and switch No. 1 closed

5. When current is flowing through the 10-ohm resistors, the voltmeter reading will be   5.____

    A. 100 volts   B. 60 volts   C. 40 volts   D. 24 volts

6. In this circuit the ammeter should have a scale range of at least zero to   6.____

    A. 1 ampere   B. 2 amperes   C. 3 amperes   D. 4 amperes

7. With the switches set for this circuit to take maximum current from the line, then the current through the fuse will be approximately   7.____

    A. 1 ampere   B. 2 amperes   C. 4 amperes   D. 10 amperes

8. The abbreviations I.D. and O.D. used in describing conduit directly refer to its   8.____

    A. diameter   B. length   C. conductivity   D. weight

9. To cut off a piece of #0000 insulated copper cable it is best to use   9.____

    A. a hacksaw   B. side-cutting pliers
    C. an electrician's knife   D. light nippers

10. Conduit is galvanized in order to   10.____

    A. improve electrical conductivity   B. protect it from corrosion
    C. obtain a smooth surface   D. insulate it

11. The best material for an electrical contact finger subjected to constant bending is   11.____

    A. brass   B. aluminum
    C. tin   D. phosphor bronze

12. One disadvantage of porcelain as an insulator is that it is   12.____

    A. only good for low voltage
    B. not satisfactory on a-c circuits
    C. a brittle material
    D. easily compressed

13. To vary the speed of a d-c motor-generator set, it would be necessary to   13.____

    A. use a rheostat in the generator field
    B. use a voltage regulator on the generator output
    C. use a rheostat in the motor field
    D. shift the brushes on the generator

14. The ordinary telephone transmitter contains granules of   14.____

    A. sulphur   B. carbon   C. borax   D. lucite

15. A stubby screwdriver is especially designed for turning screws   15.____

    A. having a damaged screw slot
    B. which are jammed tight
    C. with stripped threads
    D. inaccessible to a longer screwdriver

16. It is important to make certain a ladle does not contain water before using it to scoop up molten solder since the water may   16.____

    A. cause serious personal injury
    B. prevent the solder from sticking
    C. cool the solder
    D. dilute the solder

17. Steel helmets give workers the most protection from   17.____

    A. eye injuries   B. falling objects
    C. fire   D. electric shock

18. A slight coating of rust on small tools is best removed by   18.____

    A. applying a heavy coat of vaseline
    B. rubbing with kerosene and fine steel wool
    C. scraping with a sharp knife
    D. rubbing with a dry cloth

19. In the case of an auto-transformer, it is INCORRECT to say that   19.____

    A. the primary is insulated from the secondary
    B. a magnetic core is used
    C. a.c. is required
    D. it can be used for power purposes

20. The number 6-32 for a machine screw specifies the diameter and the   20.____

    A. length
    B. the number of threads per inch
    C. type of head
    D. hardness

21. It is undesirable to allow a soldering iron to overheat since this would cause   21.____

    A. softening of the copper tip
    B. hardening of the copper tip
    C. the soldering fumes to become poisonous
    D. damage to the tinned surface of the tip

22. To measure the small gap between relay contacts, it would be best to use a   22.____

    A. vernier caliper   B. depth gage
    C. feeler gage   D. micrometer

23. Acid is not a desirable flux to use in soldering small connections mainly because it   23.____

    A. is corrosive
    B. is expensive
    C. requires skill in handling
    D. requires a very hot iron

24. It is good practice to use standard electrician's pliers to   24.____

    A. tighten nuts
    B. remove insulation from a wire
    C. cut BX sheath
    D. shorten a wood screw

25. Three resistors having respective resistances of 12 ohms, 5 ohms, and 1 ohm are con-   25.____
nected in parallel. The combined resistance will be

    A. 18 ohms   B. 6 ohms
    C. 4 ohms   D. less than 1 ohm

26. The star drill is a multiple-pointed chisel used for drilling   26.____

    A. brass   B. stone and concrete
    C. wood   D. aluminum

27. A screwdriver in good condition should have a blade whose bottom edge is   27.____

    A. rounded   B. knife-sharp
    C. chisel-shaped   D. flat

28. From the standpoint of management, the most desirable characteristic in a newly   28.____
appointed helper would be

    A. the lack of outside personal interests
    B. the ability to keep to himself and away from the other employees
    C. the ability to satisfactorily perform his assigned duties
    D. eagerness to ask questions about all phases of the work

29. To provide transit employees with quick assistance in the case of minor injuries it would   29.____
be most logical to

    A. instruct the employees in first-aid techniques
    B. provide each employee with a first-aid kit
    C. have one centrally located medical office for the transit system
    D. equip all employees with walkie-talkie devices

30. One result of corrosion of an electrical connection is that   30.____

    A. its resistance increases
    B. its resistance decreases
    C. its temperature drops
    D. the current in the circuit increases

31. Subway cars are equipped with storage batteries. These batteries are *LEAST* likely to be   31.____
used to supply power to the car

    A. traction motors
    B. emergency lights
    C. public address system
    D. motorman-conductor communication system

32. The size of a screwdriver is defined by the   32._____

    A. length of the handle   B. thickness of the blade
    C. length of the blade   D. diameter of the handle

33. A newly appointed helper would be expected to do his work in the manner prescribed by   33._____
his foreman because

    A. it insures discipline
    B. good results are more certain with less supervision
    C. no other method would work
    D. it permits speed-up

34. When a soldered splice is covered with both rubber and friction tape, the main function of   34._____
the friction tape is to

    A. provide extra electrical insulation
    B. protect the rubber tape
    C. make the splice water-tight
    D. increase the mechanical strength of the splice

35. Powdered graphite is a good   35._____

    A. lubricant   B. abrasive   C. adhesive   D. insulator

36. A zero adjusting screw will be found on most   36._____

    A. overload relays   B. lightning arrestors
    C. voltmeters   D. switches

37. Lock nuts are frequently used in making electrical connections on terminal boards. The   37._____
purpose of the lock-nuts is to

    A. keep the connections from loosening through vibration
    B. prevent unauthorized personnel from tampering with the connections
    C. eliminate the use of flat washers
    D. increase the contact area at the connection point

38. The abbreviation D.P.D.T. used in electrical work describes a type of   38._____

    A. switch   B. motor   C. fuse   D. generator

39. A wire has a resistance of 2 ohms per 1000 feet. A piece of this wire 1500 feet long will   39._____
have a resistance of

    A. 1 ohm   B. 1.5 ohms   C. 2.5 ohms   D. 3 ohms

40. The dielectric strength of the oil used in an oil filled transformer is a direct measure of the   40._____
oil's

    A. viscosity   B. weight
    C. breakdown voltage   D. current carrying capacity

41. The power fed to a mercury arc rectifier would probably come from   41._____

    A. a rotary converter   B. a d.c.generator
    C. an a.c.source   D. a battery

42. The ordinary plug fuse has   42._____

    A. knife blade contacts   B. screw base contacts
    C. ferrule contacts   D. jack contacts

43. When using a hacksaw, it is good practice to   43._____

    A. tighten the blade in the frame by using pliers on the wing nut
    B. use heavy pressure on both the forward and return strokes
    C. slow the speed of cutting when the piece is almost cut through
    D. use very short, very rapid strokes

44. A new helper is told by an experienced helper that he is not doing a particular job prop-   44._____
erly. The best reason for the new helper to give this advice due consideration is that the
other helper

    A. has the authority to enforce his advice
    B. has more experience on the job
    C. will be resentful if his advice is not taken
    D. will not help the new man again if his advice is not taken

45. The main purpose of the oil in an oil circuit breaker is to   45._____

    A. quench the arc   B. lubricate the moving parts
    C. prevent corrosion   D. absorb moisture

46. A piece of electrical equipment which does *NOT* require a magnetic field for its operation   46._____
is

    A. a motor   B. a generator
    C. a transformer   D. an electrostatic voltmeter

47. The rating term "20-watts, 500-ohm" would generally be applied to a   47._____

    A. resistor   B. condenser
    C. switch   D. circuit breaker

48. The core of an electro-magnet is usually made of   48._____

    A. lead   B. iron   C. brass   D. bakelite

49. The A.W.G. size is used in specifying   49._____

    A. wires   B. condensers   C. switches   D. fuses

50. The metal which is preferred for use in relay contacts is   50._____

    A. brass   B. tin   C. silver   D. aluminum

KEY (CORRECT ANSWERS)

1.	A	11.	D	21.	D	31.	A	41.	C
2.	D	12.	C	22.	C	32.	C	42.	B
3.	D	13.	C	23.	A	33.	B	43.	C
4.	B	14.	B	24.	B	34.	B	44.	B
5.	D	15.	D	25.	D	35.	A	45.	A
6.	D	16.	A	26.	B	36.	C	46.	D
7.	D	17.	B	27.	D	37.	A	47.	A
8.	A	18.	B	28.	C	38.	A	48.	B
9.	A	19.	A	29.	A	39.	D	49.	A
10.	B	20.	B	30.	A	40.	C	50.	C

EXAMINATION SECTION
TEST 1

DIRECTIONS: Each question or incomplete statement is followed by several suggested answers or completions. Select the one that *BEST* answers the question or completes the statement. *PRINT THE LETTER OF THE CORRECT ANSWER IN THE SPACE AT THE RIGHT.*

1. The letters S.P.S.T. frequently found on wiring plans refer to a type of   1.____

    A. cable   B. switch   C. fuse   D. motor

2. Renewable fuses differ from ordinary fuses in that   2.____

    A. they can carry higher overloads
    B. burned out fuses can be located more easily
    C. burned out fuse elements can be readily replaced
    D. they can be used on higher voltages

3. When a maintainer reports a minor trouble orally to his foreman, the most important information the foreman would require from the maintainer would be the   3.____

    A. type of trouble and its exact location
    B. names of all men with him when he discovered the trouble
    C. exact time the trouble was discovered
    D. work he was doing when he noted the trouble

4. A helper can most quickly make himself useful on the job if he   4.____

    A. asks questions of his foreman at every opportunity
    B. continually suggests changes in work procedures to the maintainer
    C. listens carefully to instructions and carries them out
    D. insists on doing all heavy lifting himself

5. After No. 10 A.W.G., the next smaller copper wire size in common use is No.   5.____

    A. 8   B. 9   C. 11   D. 12

6. The best of the following tools to use for cutting off a piece of single-conductor #6 rubber insulated lead covered cable is a   6.____

    A. pair of electrician's pliers
    B. hacksaw
    C. hammer and cold chisel
    D. lead knife

7. Transit employees whose work requires them to enter upon the tracks in the subway are cautioned not to wear loose fitting clothing. The most important reason for this caution is that loose fitting clothing may   7.____

    A. interfere when they are using heavy tools
    B. catch on some projection of a passing train
    C. give insufficient protection against dust
    D. tear more easily than snug fitting clothing

8. It would *NOT* be good practice to tighten a one-inch hexagon nut with   8.____

    A. a monkey wrench
    B. a one-inch fixed open end wrench
    C. an adjustable open-end wrench
    D. a Stillson wrench

9. Lock washers are used principally with   9.____

    A. machine screws   B. wood screws
    C. self-tapping screws   D. lag screws

10. Toggle bolts are most appropriate for use to fasten conduit clamps to a   10.____

    A. steel column   B. concrete wall
    C. hollow tile wall   D. brick wall

11. If a 10-24 by 3/4" machine screw is not available, the screw which could be most easily   11.____
modified to use in an emergency is a

    A. 10-24 by 1/2"   B. 12-24 by 3/4"
    C. 10-24 by 1 1/2"   D. 8-24 by 3/4"

12. Lighting in many of the subway cars is provided by 22 lamps all connected in a single   12.____
series circuit which is fed from the third rail at 600 volts. The voltage rating of each indi-
vidual lamp in the series must be approximately

    A. 600 volts   B. 120 volts
    C. 30 volts   D. 22 volts

13. In attempting to revive a person who has stopped breathing after receiving an electric   13.____
shock, it is most important to

    A. start artificial respiration immediately
    B. wrap the victim in a blanket
    C. massage the ankles and wrists
    D. force the victim to swallow a stimulant

14. After pulling the fuse of a 600-volt circuit, and before starting the work of connecting   14.____
additional equipment to the circuit, the most important safety precaution to take is to

    A. examine the condition of the fuse
    B. disconnect all load from the circuit
    C. check that all tools have insulated handles
    D. test to make sure the circuit is dead

15. The most practical way to determine in the field if a large coil of #14 wire has the required   15.____
length for a given job is to

    A. weigh the coil and compare with a new 1000-foot coil
    B. measure the electrical resistance and compare with a 1000-foot coil
    C. measure the length of one turn and multiply by the number of turns
    D. unwind the coil and lay the wire alongside the conduit before pulling it in

16. Maintainers of the transit system are required to report defective equipment to their superiors, even when the maintenance of the particular equipment is handled entirely by another bureau. The purpose of this rule is to

    16.____

    A. fix responsibility
    B. discourage slackers
    C. encourage alertness
    D. prevent accidents

17. A standard pipe thread differs from a standard screw thread in that the pipe thread

    17.____

    A. is tapered
    B. is deeper
    C. requires no lubrication when cutting
    D. has the same pitch for any diameter of pipe

18. The material which is LEAST likely to be found in use as the outer covering of rubber insulated wires or cables is

    18.____

    A. cotton
    B. varnished cambric
    C. lead
    D. neoprene

19. In measuring to determine the size of a stranded insulated conductor, the proper place to use the wire gauge is on

    19.____

    A. the insulation
    B. the outer covering
    C. the stranded conductor
    D. one strand of the conductor

20. Rubber insulation on an electrical conductor would most quickly be damaged by continuous contact with

    20.____

    A. acid
    B. water
    C. oil
    D. alkali

21. If a fuse clip becomes hot under normal circuit load, the most probable cause is that the

    21.____

    A. clip makes poor contact with the fuse ferrule
    B. circuit wires are too small
    C. current rating of the fuse is too high
    D. voltage rating of the fuse is too low

22. If the input to a 10 to 1 step-down transformer is 15 amperes at 2400 volts, the secondary output would be nearest to

    22.____

    A. 1.5 amperes at 24,000 volts
    B. 150 amperes at 240 volts
    C. 1.5 amperes at 240 volts
    D. 150 amperes at 24,000 volts

23. The resistance of a copper wire to the flow of electricity

    23.____

    A. increases as the diameter of the wire increases
    B. decreases as the diameter of the wire decreases
    C. decreases as the length of the wire increases
    D. increases as the length of the wire increases

24. Where galvanized steel conduit is used, the primary purpose of the galvanizing is to 24.___

    A. increase mechanical strength
    B. retard rusting
    C. provide a good surface for painting
    D. provide good electrical contact for grounding

25. The lamps used for station and tunnel lighting in the subways are generally operated at 25.___
slightly less than their rated voltage. The logical reason for this is to

    A. prevent overloading of circuits
    B. increase the life of the lamps
    C. decrease glare
    D. obtain a more even distribution of light

26. The correct method of measuring the power taken by an a.c. electric motor is to use a 26.___

    A. wattmeter
    B. voltmeter and an ammeter
    C. power factor meter
    D. tachometer

27. Assume that you have been asked to get the tools for a maintainer to use in taking down 27.___
a run of exposed conduit (including outlet boxes) from its installed location on the surface
of a concrete wall. The combination of tools which would probably prove most useful
would be a

    A. Stillson wrench, a box wrench, and a hack saw
    B. hack saw, a screw driver, and an adjustable open-end wrench
    C. screw driver, an adjustable open-end wrench, and a Stillson wrench
    D. screw driver, a hammer, and a box wrench

Questions 28 - 37.
Questions 28 through 37 refer to the use of the tools shown on the next page. Read the item and, for the operation given, select the proper tool to be used from those shown. PRINT, in the correspondingly numbered item space at the right, the letter given below your selected tool.

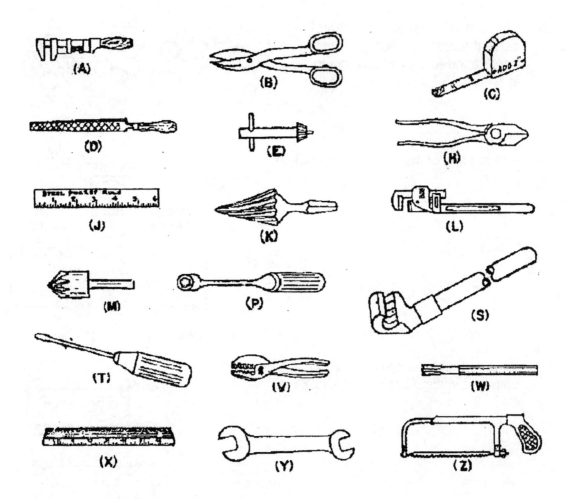

(A)   (B)   (C)

(D)   (E)   (H)

(J)   (K)   (L)

(M)   (P)   (S)

(T)   (V)   (W)

(X)   (Y)   (Z)

28. Loosening the nut holding a wire on a stud terminal.   28._____

29. Removing burrs from the inner edge of conduit after cutting it.   29._____

30. Measuring the distance between exposed terminals on a low-voltage switchboard which   30._____
    is alive.

31. Loosening a coupling which is tight on the end of a piece of conduit.   31._____

32. Tightening the chuck on an electric drill.   32._____

33. Tightening a 3/4 inch conduit bushing inside an outlet box.   33._____

34. Skinning a no. 14 A.W.G. rubber insulated wire.   34._____

35. Cutting off part of a brass machine screw which is too long.   35._____

36. Prying off a rubber gasket that is stuck to the inside of the cover that has been taken off a   36._____
    watertight pull box.

37. Making a hole for a lead anchor in a concrete wall.   37._____

38. The sketch which correctly repre- sents the cross-section of a stan- dard stranded copper con- ductor is

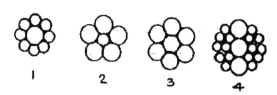

A. 1   B. 2   C. 3   D. 4

38.____

39. The reading of the voltmeter should be

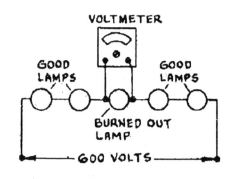

A. 600   B. 300   C. 120   D. zero

39.____

40. If the voltage of each of the dry cells shown is 1.5 volts, the voltage between X and Y is
    A. 3
    B. 6
    C. 9
    D. 12

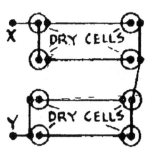

40.____

41. In accordance with the voltages shown, the power supply must be
    A. three-wire d.c.
    B. three-phase a.c.
    C. two-phase a.c.
    D. single-phase a.c.

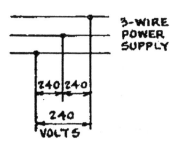

41.____

42. Meter 1 is
    A. an ammeter
    B. a frequency meter
    C. a wattmeter
    D. a voltmeter

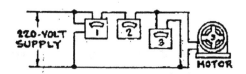

42.____

43. The insulator shown is a
    A. pin type insulator
    B. strain insulator
    C. suspension type insulator
    D. insulating bushing

43.____

44. The two coils are wound in the directions indicated and both coils have exactly the same number of turns. When the switch is closed, the north pole of the permanent magnet will be
    A. repelled by both the left-hand and right-hand cores
    B. attracted by both the left-hand and right-hand cores
    C. attracted by the left-hand core and repelled by the right-hand core
    D. repelled by the left-hand core and attracted by the right-hand core

44.____

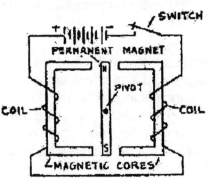

45. Regardless of the battery voltage, it is clear that the smallest current is in the resistor having a resistance of
    A. 200 ohms
    B. 300 ohms
    C. 400 ohms
    D. 500 ohms

45.____

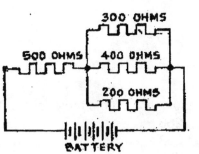

46. The five lamps shown are each rated at 120-volts 60-watts. If all are good lamps, lamp no. 5 will be
    A. much brighter than normal
    B. about its normal brightness
    C. much dimmer than normal
    D. completely dark

46.____

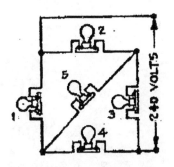

47. If the voltmeter reads 34 volts, the circuit voltage is about
    A. 68
    B. 85
    C. 102
    D. 119

47.____

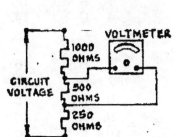

48. If the voltage of the supply is 120 volts, the readings of the voltmeter should be
   A. 60 volts on each meter
   B. 120 volts on each meter
   C. 80 volts on meter #1 and 40 volts on meter #2
   D. 80 volts on meter #2 and 40 volts on meter #1

48.____

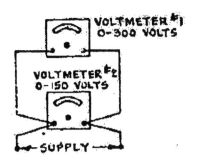

49. The sketch shows the four resistance dials and the multiplying dial of a resistance bridge. The four resistance dials can be set to any value of resistance up to 10,000 ohms, and the multiplier can be set at any of the nine points shown. In their present positions, the five pointers indicate a reading of
   A. 13.60
   B. 136,000
   C. 130,600
   D. 13.06

49.____

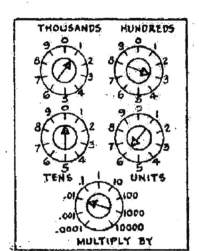

50. The indication on the meter scale is
   A. 266
   B. 258
   C. 253
   D. 251.5

50.____

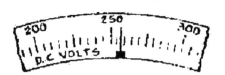

KEY (CORRECT ANSWERS)

1.	B	11.	C	21.	A	31.	L	41.	B
2.	C	12.	C	22.	B	32.	E	42.	C
3.	A	13.	A	23.	D	33.	V	43.	A
4.	C	14.	D	24.	B	34.	H	44.	A
5.	D	15.	C	25.	B	35.	H	45.	C
6.	B	16.	D	26.	A	36.	T	46.	D
7.	B	17.	A	27.	C	37.	W	47.	D
8.	D	18.	B	28.	P	38.	C	48.	B
9.	A	19.	D	29.	K	39.	A	49.	D
10.	C	20.	C	30.	X	40.	B	50.	B

TEST 2

DIRECTIONS: Each question or incomplete statement is followed by several suggested answers or completions. Select the one that *BEST* answers the question or completes the statement. *PRINT THE LETTER OF THE CORRECT ANSWER IN THE SPACE AT THE RIGHT.*

1. The reading of the kilowatt-hour meter is
   A. 7972
   B. 2786
   C. 1786
   D. 6872

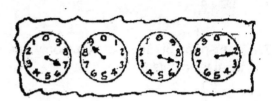

1._____

2. The reading shown on the micrometer is
   A. 0.203
   B. 0.222
   C. 0.228
   D. 0.247

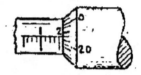

2._____

3. The center to center distance between the two poles is

   A. $\dfrac{11"}{16}$

   B. $1\dfrac{1"}{16}$

   C. $1\dfrac{11"}{16}$

   D. $1\dfrac{13"}{16}$

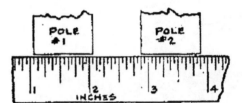

3._____

4. The outlet which will accept the plug is
   A. 1
   B. 2
   C. 3
   D. 4

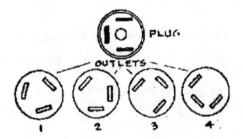

4._____

5. The double-pole double-throw switch which is properly connected as a reversing switch is
   A. 1
   B. 2
   C. 3
   D. 4

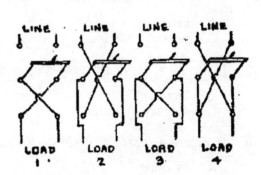

5._____

99

6. The standard coupling for rigid electrical conduit is
   A. 1
   B. 2
   C. 3
   D. 4

6.____

7. The shape of nut most commonly used on electrical terminals is
   A. 1
   B. 2
   C. 3
   D. 4

7.____

8. The stove bolt is
   A. 1
   B. 2
   C. 3
   D. 4

8.____

Questions 9 - 14.
Questions 9 through 14 refer to the figures on the following page.
Each item gives the proper figure to use with that item.

9. Referring to Figure 1, if the 500-ohm resistor becomes open circuited, the reading of the ammeter will probably

9.____

   A. remain unchanged   B. decrease
   C. increase   D. drop to zero

10. The total equivalent resistance in ohms between points X and Y in Figure 2 is

10.____

   A. 3   B. 5   C. 15   D. 45

11. The reading of the voltmeter in Figure 3 should be

11.____

   A. 150   B. 100   C. 50   D. zero

12. In Figure 4, if switch 1 only is closed the reading of the voltmeter will

12.____

   A. increase   B. decrease, but not to zero
   C. remain unchanged   D. become zero

13. In Figure 4, if switch 2 only is closed the reading of the voltmeter will

13.____

   A. increase   B. decrease, but not to zero
   C. remain unchanged   D. become zero

14. In Figure 4, if switch 3 only is closed the reading of the voltmeter will

14.____

   A. increase   B. decrease, but not to zero
   C. remain unchanged   D. become zero

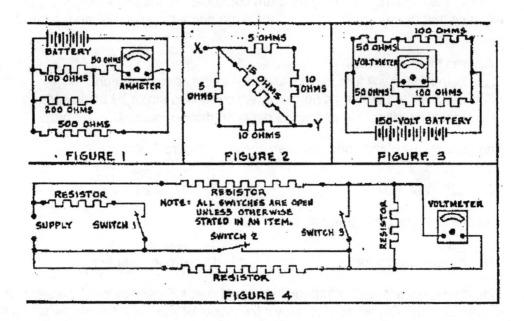

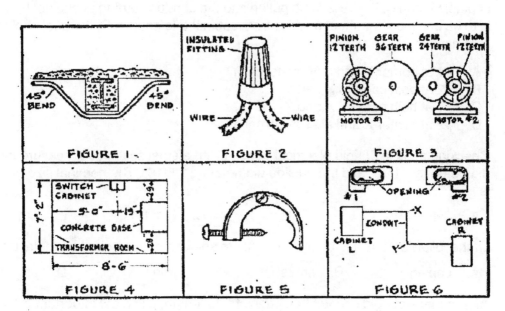

Questions 15 - 20.

Questions 15 through 20 refer to the figures above. Each item gives the proper figure to use with that item.

15. When a wire is pulled into the conduit in Figure 1, it must go around bends amounting to a total of

15.____

   A. 0°   B. 90°   C. 180°   D. 360°

16. Wires are often spliced by the use of a fitting like the one shown in Figure 2. The use of this fitting does away with the need for

16.____

   A. skinning   B. cleaning
   C. twisting   D. soldering

17. The two identical motors in Figure 3 are connected to the same power supply and are wired so that they normally tend to turn in the same direction. When the power is turned on

    A. the motors will stall
    B. both motors will turn at normal speed in the same direction
    C. motor #1 will turn in its normal direction driving motor #2 backwards
    D. motor #2 will turn in its normal direction driving motor #1 backwards

17.____

18. The dimensions of the concrete base shown in Figure 4 are

    A. 14" x 28"   B. 23" x 28"
    C. 23" x 29"   D. 14" x 29"

18.____

19. The device shown in Figure 5 is a

    A. C-clamp   B. test clip
    C. battery connector D. ground clamp

19.____

20. Figure 6 shows two types of conduit fitting (#1 and #2) used as pull boxes at sharp bends in conduit runs. The figure also shows the layout of a conduit run on the wall between cabinets L and R. If wire is to be pulled into the conduit starting at cabinet L, and the wire is to be continuous without a splice from cabinet L to cabinet R, the best choice of fittings is to have a

    A. #1 at corner X and a #2 at corner Y
    B. #2 at both corners X and Y
    C. #1 at both corners X and Y
    D. #2 at corner X and a #1 at corner Y

20.____

21. Checking a piece of rigid electrical conduit with a steel scale, you measure the inside diameter as 1 1/16" and the outside diameter as 1 5/16". The nominal size of this conduit is

    A. 3/4"   B. 1"   C. C 1 1/4"   D. D 1 1/2"

21.____

22. Of the following, it would be most difficult to solder a copper wire to a metal plate made of

    A. copper   B. brass   C. iron   D. tin

22.____

23. After a piece of rigid conduit has been cut. to length, it is most important to

    A. ream the inside edge to prevent injury to wires
    B. file the end flat to make an accurate fit
    C. coat the cut surface with red lead to prevent rust
    D. file the outside edge to a taper for ease in threading

23.____

24. When lamps on the transit system are installed at less than 7 ft. 6 in. from the floor, they are provided with lamp guards. The purpose of guards in such cases is most likely to

    A. reduce glare
    B. prevent accidental burning of passengers
    C. minimize lamp breakage
    D. discourage lamp thefts

24.____

25. Rigid conduit is generally secured to sheet metal outlet boxes by means of   25.____

     A. threadless couplings   B. box connectors
     C. locknuts and bushings   D. conduit clamps

26. According to generally recommended practice, helper Richard Roe answering the tele-   26.____
phone at the Undercliff Ave. signal section headquarters would do best to say

     A. "Hello, this is Undercliff Ave., Roe speaking."
     B. "This is Roe, -Signal Section."
     C. "Roe, Signal Section, -Who's calling?"
     D. "Signal Section, Undercliff Ave., Roe speaking."

27. While a certain d.c. shunt motor is driving a light load, part of the field winding becomes   27.____
short circuited. The motor will most likely

     A. increase its speed
     B. decrease its speed
     C. remain at the same speed
     D. come to a stop

28. The circumference of a circle is given by the formula $C = 2\pi R$, where C is the circumfer-   28.____
ence, R is the radius, and π is approximately 3 1/7. The circumference of an oil drum
having a diameter of one foot and nine inches is therefore about

     A. 132 inches   B. 66 inches
     C. 33 inches   D. 17 inches

29. Each time a certain electric heater is turned on, the incandescent lights connected to the   29.____
same branch circuit become dimmer and when the heater is turned off the lamps
become brighter. The factor which probably contributes most to this effect is the

     A. voltage of the circuit
     B. size of the circuit fuse
     C. current taken by the lamps
     D. size of the circuit conductors

30. Comparing the shunt field winding with the series field winding of a compound d.c. motor,   30.____
it would be correct to say that the shunt field winding has

     A. more turns but the lower resistance
     B. more turns and the higher resistance
     C. fewer turns and the lower resistance
     D. fewer turns but the higher resistance

Questions 31 - 37.
Questions 31 through 37 are based on the motor inspection instructions given below. Read
these instructions carefully before answering these questions.

GENERAL INSTRUCTIONS FOR WEEKLY MOTOR INSPECTION

Inspect each motor to see if there is any unusual amount of dust or chips on or near it, and to see if there is anything left lying about which might interfere with the free running or ventilation of the motor. Check lubrication in accordance with standard instructions for the type of motor. At the same time, take notice of any unusual noise or odor for evidence of excessive wear or overloading; feel bearing housings for heat and vibration. Inspect the commutator of each d.c. motor for discoloration, dirt, and uneven wear; look for sparking at the brushes while the motor is running.

Any minor defect should be corrected on the spot as soon as it is discovered, and the proper report made to your superior of the action taken. Any major defect that is found should be reported promptly to your superior so that it can be corrected before the damage becomes too great to be repaired.

31. One sure sign that there has been sparking at the brushes of a stopped d.c. motor would be   31.____

    A. the odor of hot rubber insulation
    B. hot bearings
    C. grooves worn around the commutator
    D. pits on the commutator surface

32. A common way of reducing the chances of uneven commutator wear is to   32.____

    A. use brushes of different hardness
    B. allow some end play in the motor bearings
    C. anneal the commutator after assembly
    D. turn the commutator down frequently

33. Upon entering a pump room in which a motor-driven pump is running, the maintainer detects the odor of hot insulating varnish. This odor indicates that the   33.____

    A. varnish has been freshly applied
    B. bearings are poorly lubricated
    C. room is insufficiently ventilated
    D. motor is being overloaded

34. If an unusual amount of dust is found around the base of a motor which is being inspected, the proper procedure to follow is to   34.____

    A. take no action but report the motor for further inspection
    B. remove the dust and note the action in your daily report
    C. inspect the bearings for signs of excessive wear
    D. lubricate the motor in accordance with standard instructions

35. If one bearing housing of a running motor feels exceptionally hot but there is no unusual vibration, the most logical conclusion is that the   35.____

    A. motor is being overloaded
    B. bearing needs lubrication
    C. shaft has become worn
    D. motor has been running a long time

36. During a weekly inspection, the motor driving a certain drainage pump is found to be unusually noisy when it runs. The starting and stopping of this motor is automatically controlled by a float switch. In order to comply with the above general instructions, the

    A. cause should be investigated and the condition reported promptly to your superior for corrective action
    B. float switch should be adjusted so that the motor will run less frequently
    C. motor should be shut down immediately
    D. bearings should be lubricated in accordance with standard instructions

36.____

37. When making a weekly motor inspection you would be *LEAST* likely to need a

    A. grease gun   B. dust brush
    C. thermometer   D. flashlight

37.____

38. The most important reason for using a fuse-puller when removing a cartridge fuse from the fuse clips is to

    A. prevent blowing of the fuse
    B. prevent injury to the fuse element
    C. reduce the chances of personal injury
    D. reduce arcing at the fuse clips

38.____

39. A coil of wire wound on an iron core draws exactly 5 amperes when connected across the terminals of a ten-volt storage battery. If this coil is now connected across the ten-volt secondary terminals of an ordinary power transformer, the current drawn will be

    A. less than 5 amperes
    B. more than 5 amperes
    C. exactly 5 amperes
    D. more or less than 5 amperes depending on the frequency

39.____

40. Standard iron conduit comes in 10-foot lengths. The number of such lengths required for a run of 23 yards is

    A. 3   B. 4   C. 6   D. 7

40.____

41. A revolution counter applied to the end of a rotating shaft reads 100 when a stop-watch is started. It reads 850 when the stop-watch indicates 90 seconds. The average RPM of the shaft is

    A. 8.4   B. 9.4   C. 500   D. 567

41.____

42. Motor speeds are generally measured directly in RPM by the use of a

    A. potentiometer   B. manometer
    C. dynamometer   D. tachometer

42.____

43. A rule of the transit system is that the system telephones must not be used for personal calls. The most important reason for this rule is that such personal calls

    A. increase telephone maintenance
    B. tie up telephones which may be urgently needed for company business
    C. waste company time
    D. require additional operators

43.____

44. To reverse the direction of rotation of a 3-phase motor, it is necessary to 44.____

    A. increase the resistance of the rotor circuit
    B. interchange any two of the three line connections
    C. interchange all three line connections
    D. reverse the polarity of the rotor circuit

45. Mica is commonly used in electrical construction for 45.____

    A. commutator bar separators
    B. switchboard panels
    C. strain insulators
    D. heater cord insulation

46. The rating term "1000 ohms, 10 watts" would generally be applied to a 46.____

    A. heater   B. relay   C. resistor   D. transformer

47. According to the National Electrical Code, the identified (or grounded) conductor of the branch circuit supplying an incandescent lamp socket must be connected to the screw shell. The most likely reason for this requirement is that 47.____

    A. longer lamp life results
    B. the wiring will be kept more nearly uniform
    C. persons are more likely to come in contact with the shell
    D. the shell can carry heavier currents

48. In an installation used to charge a storage battery from a motor-generator you would LEAST expect to find 48.____

    A. a rectifier   B. a rheostat
    C. a voltmeter   D. an ammeter

49. The letters R.I.L.C. are used in identifying 49.____

    A. transformers   B. motors
    C. cables   D. storage batteries

50. Two separate adjacent lamp bulbs are placed behind each colored lens of the train signals alongside the tracks in the subway. The logical reason why two bulbs are used instead of one bulb is to 50.____

    A. permit lower line voltage
    B. increase the light intensity
    C. permit the use of smaller bulbs
    D. keep the signal lighted in case one bulb fails

———————

KEY (CORRECT ANSWERS)

1. D	11. D	21. B	31. D	41. C
2. B	12. C	22. C	32. B	42. D
3. D	13. A	23. A	33. D	43. B
4. C	14. D	24. D	34. B	44. B
5. B	15. C	25. C	35. B	45. A
6. A	16. D	26. D	36. A	46. C
7. B	17. A	27. A	37. C	47. C
8. C	18. B	28. B	38. C	48. A
9. C	19. D	29. D	39. A	49. C
10. B	20. D	30. B	40. D	50. D

———————

EXAMINATION SECTION
TEST 1

DIRECTIONS: Each question or incomplete statement is followed by several suggested answers or completions. Select the one that *BEST* answers the question or completes the statement. *PRINT THE LETTER OF THE CORRECT ANSWER IN THE SPACE AT THE RIGHT.*

1. Employees of the transit system are cautioned, as a safety measure, not to use water to extinguish fires involving electrical equipment. One logical reason for this caution is that the water

    A.   may transmit electrical shock to the user
    B.   may crack hot insulation
    C.   will not extinguish a fire started by electricity
    D.   will cause harmful steam

1.____

2. As compared with solid wire, stranded wire of the same gage size is

    A.   given a higher current rating
    B.   easier to skin
    C.   larger in total diameter
    D.   better for high voltage

2.____

3. When drilling holes in concrete from the top of an extension ladder, it is *LEAST* important to

    A.   wear goggles
    B.   wear gloves
    C.   hook one leg through the rung of the ladder
    D.   wear a helmet

3.____

4. Motor frames are usually positively grounded by a special connection in order to

    A.   remove static   B.   protect against lightning
    C.   provide a neutral   D.   protect against shock

4.____

5. If a live conductor is contacted accidentally, the severity of the electrical shock is determined primarily by

    A.   the size of the conductor
    B.   whether the current is a.c. or d.c.
    C.   the contact resistance
    D.   the current in the conductor

5.____

Items 6-15.

Items 6 through 15 in Column I are electrical equipment parts each of which is commonly made from one of the materials listed in Column II. For each part in Column I, select the most appropriate material from Column II. *PRINT,* in the correspondingly numbered item space at the right, the letter given beside your selected material.

COLUMN I	COLUMN II
(electrical equipment parts)	(materials)

6. d.c. circuit breaker arcing-tips   A. copper   6._____

7. cartridge fuse casing   B. silver   7._____

8. pig-tail jumpers for contacts   C. porcelain   8._____

9. commutator bars   D. carbon   9._____

10. bearing oil-rings   E. transite   10._____

11. cores for wound heater-coils   H. wood   11._____

12. center contact in screw lamp-sockets   J. lead   12._____

13. acid storage battery terminals   K. brass   13._____

14. arc chutes   L. phosphor bronze   14._____

15. operating sticks for disconnecting switches   M. fiber   15._____

16. One of the rules of the transit system prohibits "horseplay". For electrical employees, this rule is most important because   16._____

A. horseplay wastes company time
B. electrical work does not permit relaxation at any time
C. electrical work is very complicated
D. men are liable to injury when so engaged

17. If a snap switch rated at 5 amperes is used for an electric heater which draws 10 amperes, the most likely result is that the   17._____

A. circuit fuse will be blown
B. circuit wiring will become hot
C. heater output will be halved
D. switch contacts will become hot

18. If you are assigned by your foreman to a job which you do not understand, you should   18._____

A. explain and request further instructions from your foreman
B. try to do the job because you learn from experience
C. do the job to the best of your ability as that is all that can be expected
D. ask another foreman since your foreman should have explained the job when it was assigned

19. In carrying a length of conduit through a reasonably crowded subway station, a maintainer and his helper would follow the best procedure if   19._____

A. the helper held one end and the maintainer the other at arm's length downward
B. the helper carried it near the middle and the maintainer went ahead to warn passengers

   C.   each employee carried one end on his shoulder
   D.   the two employees carry at the 1/3 and 2/3 points respectively

20.   To straighten a long length of wire, which has been tightly coiled, before pulling it into a   20.____
conduit run, a good method is to

   A.   roll the wire into a coil in the opposite direction
   B.   fasten one end to the floor and whip it against the floor from the other end
   C.   draw it over a convenient edge
   D.   hold the wire at one end and twist it with the pliers from the other end

21.   The 110-volt bus supplying the control power in a substation is often d.c. from storage   21.____
batteries charged automatically rather than a.c. from a transformer using the a.c. main
supply. One reason is that the d.c. system

   A.   requires less maintenance
   B.   is more reliable
   C.   requires less power
   D.   permits smaller control wires

22.   Mercury arc rectifiers are often used rather than rotary converters in above-ground sub-   22.____
stations in residential areas because they are

   A.   cooler   B.   less dangerous
   C.   smaller   D.   less noisy

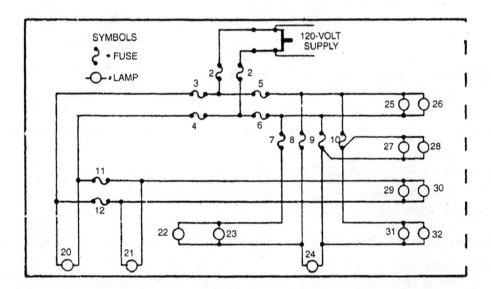

Items 23 - 31.

Items 23 through 31 are based on the above wiring diagram. All of the lamps are normally
lighted. These items in Column I are descriptions of abnormal conditions each of which is
caused by one of the faults listed in Column II. *PRINT*, in the correspondingly numbered item
space at the right, the letter given beside your selected fault.

Column I (abnormal conditions)		Column II (faults)	
23.	Lamp Nos. 24, 27, 28, 31, and 32 dark	A. Either fuse #11 or fuse #12 blown	23.____
24.	Lamp Nos. 27, 28, 31, and 32 dark	B. Fuse #9 blown	24.____
25.	Lamp Nos. 21, 29, and 30 dark	C. Fuse #10 blown	25.____
26.	Lamp Nos. 22 and 23 dark	D. Lamp burned out	26.____
27.	Only lamp No. 24 dark	E. Either fuse #9 or fuse #10 blown	27.____
28.	Lamp Nos. 20, 21, 29, and 30 dark	H. Either fuse #5 or fuse #6 blown	28.____
29.	Lamp Nos. 22, 23, and 24 dark	J. Fuse #8 blown	29.____
		K. Fuse #7 blown	
30.	Lamp Nos. 22, 23, 24, 25, 26, 27, 28, 31, and 32 dark	L. Either fuse #3 or fuse #4 blown	30.____
31.	Only lamp No. 20 dark	M. Either fuse #1 or fuse #2 blown	31.____

32. The wire size most commonly used for branch circuits in residences is   32.____

    A. #14   B. #16   C. #12   D. #18

33. If the applied voltage on an incandescent lamp is increased 10%, the lamp will   33.____

    A. have a longer life
    B. consume less power
    C. burn more brightly
    D. fail by insulation breakdown

34. You would expect that the overload trip coil on an ordinary air circuit breaker would have   34.____

    A. heavy wire   B. fine wire
    C. many turns   D. heavily insulated wire

35. A cycle counter is an electrical timer which, when energized by alternating current,   35.____
counts the number of cycles until it is deenergized. If a cycle counter is energized from a
60-cycle power supply for ten seconds, the reading of the instrument should be

    A. 6   B. 10   C. 60   D. 600

36. Artificial respiration should be administered to the victim of electric shock ONLY if he is   36.____
NOT

    A. conscious   B. bleeding
    C. breathing   D. burned

37. A rule of the transit system states that, "In walking on the track, walk opposite the direction of traffic on that track if possible". By logical reasoning, the principal safety idea behind this rule is that the man on the track

    A. is more likely to see an approaching train
    B. will be seen more readily by the motorman
    C. need not be as careful
    D. is better able to judge the speed of the train

37.____

38. The most practical way to determine in the field if a large coil of #14 wire has the required length for a given job is to

    A. weigh the coil
    B. measure one turn and count the turns
    C. unroll it into another coil
    D. make a visual comparison with a full coil

38.____

39. A frequency meter is constructed as a potential device, that is, to be connected across the line. A logical reason for this is that

    A. only the line voltage has frequency
    B. a transformer may then be used with it
    C. the reading will be independent of the varying current
    D. it is safer than a series device

39.____

40. If you feel that one of your co-workers is not doing his share of the work, your best procedure is to

    A. point this out to the foreman
    B. reduce your output to bring the matter to a head
    C. increase your own output as a good example
    D. take no action and continue to do your job properly

40.____

41. It is usually not safe to connect 110 volts d.c. to a magnet coil designed for 110 volts a.c. because the

    A. insulation is insufficient
    B. iron may overheat
    C. wire may overheat
    D. inductance may be too high

41.____

42. The most satisfactory temporary replacement for a 40-watt, 120-volt incandescent lamp, if an identical replacement is not available, is a lamp rated at

    A. 100 watts, 240 volts   B. 60 watts, 130 volts
    C. 40 watts, 32 volts   D. 15 watts, 120 volts

42.____

43. If the following bare copper wire sizes were arranged in the order of increasing weight per 1000 feet, the correct arrangement would be

    A. #00, #40, #8   B. #40, #00, #8
    C. #00, #8, #40   D. #40, #8, #00

43.____

44. The purpose of having a rheostat in the field circuit of a d.c. shunt motor is to   44._____

  A. control the speed of the motor
  B. minimize the starting current
  C. limit the field current to a safe value
  D. reduce sparking at the brushes

45. If the maintainer to whom you are assigned gives you a job to be done in a certain way   45._____
    and, after starting the job, you think of another method which you are convinced is better,
    you should

  A. follow the procedure given by the maintainer since he most likely would insist on
     his method anyhow
  B. request his opinion of your method before proceeding further
  C. try your own method since the maintainer probably will not know the difference
  D. inform the foreman next time he comes around

46. The resistance of a 1000-ft. length of a certain size copper wire is required to be 10.0   46._____
    ohms $\pm$ 2%. This wire would NOT be acceptable if the resistance was

  A. 10.12 ohms   B. 10.02 ohms
  C. 10.22 ohms   D. 9.82 ohms

47. The LEAST important action in making a good soldered connection between two wires is   47._____
    to

  A. use the proper flux   B. clean the wires well
  C. use plenty of solder   D. use sufficient heat

48. When you are newly assigned as a helper to an experienced maintainer, he is most likely   48._____
    to give you good training if your attitude is that

  A. he is responsible for your progress
  B. he should do the jobs where little is to be learned
  C. you need the benefit of his experience
  D. you have the basic knowledge but lack the details

49. According to the rules, electrical maintainers must not permit other employees to replace 49._____
    lamps of authorized wattage with lamps of higher wattage in the working areas of such
    employees. The most likely reason for this rule is

  A. to prevent such employees from injuring their eyes
  B. that higher wattage lamps cost more
  C. to avoid overloading lighting circuits
  D. to keep the cost of electricity down

50. In the subway system, it would be most logical to expect to find floodlights located in the 50._____

  A. under-river tunnels
  B. outdoor train storage yards
  C. section maintenance headquarters
  D. subway storage rooms

KEY (CORRECT ANSWERS)

1. A	11. C	21. B	31. D	41. C
2. C	12. L	22. D	32. A	42. B
3. D	13. J	23. B	33. C	43. D
4. D	14. E	24. C	34. A	44. A
5. C	15. H	25. A	35. D	45. B
6. D	16. D	26. K	36. C	46. C
7. M	17. D	27. D	37. A	47. C
8. A	18. A	28. L	38. B	48. C
9. A	19. A	29. J	39. C	49. C
10. K	20. B	30. H	40. D	50. B

TEST 2

DIRECTIONS: Each question or incomplete statement is followed by several suggested answers or completions. Select the one that *BEST* answers the question or completes the statement. *PRINT THE LETTER OF THE CORRECT ANSWER IN THE SPACE AT THE RIGHT.*

1. Of the following, the best conductor of electricity is   1.____

   A. tungsten   B. iron   C. aluminum   D. carbon

2. A 600-volt cartridge fuse is most readily distinguished from a 250-volt cartridge fuse of   2.____
   the same ampere rating by comparing the

   A. insulating materials used
   B. shape of the ends
   C. diameters
   D. lengths

3. When carrying conduit, employees are cautioned against lifting with the fingers inserted   3.____
   in the end. The probable reason for this caution is to avoid the possibility of

   A. dropping and damaging the conduit
   B. getting dirt or perspiration inside
   C. cutting the fingers on the edge of the conduit
   D. straining finger muscles

4. Many power-transformer cases are filled with oil. The purpose of the oil is to   4.____

   A. prevent rusting of the core
   B. reduce a-c hum
   C. insulate the coils from the case
   D. transmit heat from the coils and core case

5. In order to make certain that a 600 volt circuit is dead V. before working on it, the best   5.____
   procedure is to

   A. test with a voltmeter
   B. "short" the circuit quickly with a piece of insulated wire
   C. see if any of the insulated conductors are warm
   D. disconnect one of the wires of the circuit near the feed

6. Electrical maintainers in the transit system are generally instructed in first aid in case of   6.____
   electrical shock. The most likely reason for this procedure is to

   A. decrease the number of accidents
   B. provide temporary emergency aid
   C. eliminate the need for calling a doctor
   D. reduce the necessity for "killing" circuits for maintenance

7. When closing an exposed knife switch on a panel, the action should be positive and rapid   7.____
   because there is less likelihood of

   A. the operator receiving a shock
   B. the operator being burned

    C.   the fuse blowing
    D.   injury to equipment connected to the circuit

8.   Lubrication is *NEVER* used on   8.____

    A.   a knife switch
    B.   a die when threading conduit
    C.   wires being pulled into a conduit
    D.   a commutator

9.   If one plug fuse in a 110-volt circuit blows because of a short-circuit, a 110-volt lamp   9.____
   screwed into the fuse socket will

    A.   burn dimly   B.   remain dark
    C.   burn out   D.   burn normally

10.   Of the following, the *LEAST* undesirable practice if a specified wire size is not available   10.____
   for part of a circuit is to

    A.   use two wires of 1/2 capacity in parallel as a substitute
    B.   use the next larger size wire
    C.   use a smaller size wire if the length is short
    D.   reduce the size of the fuse and use smaller wire

11.   If it is necessary to increase slightly the tension of an ordinary coiled spring in a relay, the   11.____
   proper procedure is to

    A.   cut off one or two turns
    B.   compress it slightly
    C.   stretch it slightly
    D.   unhook one end, twist and replace

12.   The most important reason for insisting on neatness in maintenance quarters is that it   12.____

    A.   makes a good impression on visitors and officials
    B.   decreases the chances of accidents to employees
    C.   provides jobs to fill the unavoidable gaps in daily routine
    D.   prevents tools from becoming rusty

Items 13-21.

Items 13 through 21 in Column I are wiring devices each of which properly would be used at one of the locations indicated by a large dot (●) on one of the four sketches shown in Column II. For each device in Column I, select the suitable location from Column II. *PRINT,* in the correspondingly numbered item space at the right, the letter given beside your selected location.

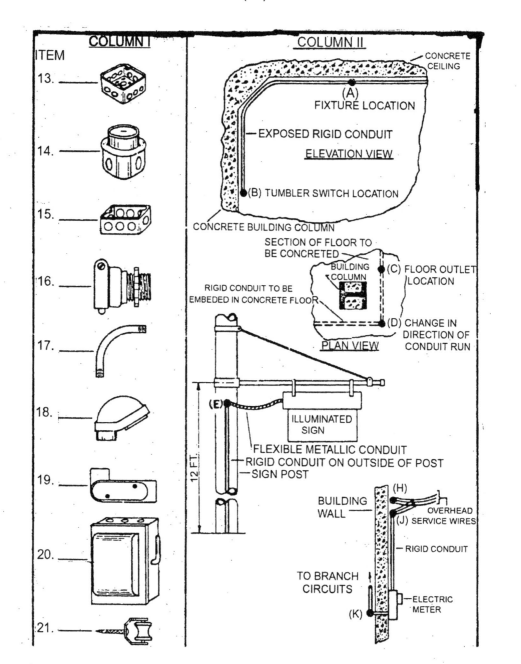

COLUMN I	COLUMN II

ITEM

13. _____

14. _____

15. _____

16. _____

17. _____

18. _____

19. _____

20. _____

21. _____

CONCRETE CEILING

(A) FIXTURE LOCATION

EXPOSED RIGID CONDUIT

ELEVATION VIEW

(B) TUMBLER SWITCH LOCATION

CONCRETE BUILDING COLUMN

SECTION OF FLOOR TO BE CONCRETED

BUILDING COLUMN

(C) FLOOR OUTLET LOCATION

RIGID CONDUIT TO BE EMBEDED IN CONCRETE FLOOR

(D) CHANGE IN DIRECTION OF CONDUIT RUN

PLAN VIEW

(E)

ILLUMINATED SIGN

FLEXIBLE METALLIC CONDUIT
RIGID CONDUIT ON OUTSIDE OF POST
SIGN POST

12 FT.

BUILDING WALL

(H)

OVERHEAD
(J) SERVICE WIRES

RIGID CONDUIT

TO BRANCH CIRCUITS

ELECTRIC METER

(K)

13. _____

14. _____

15. _____

16. _____

17. _____

18. _____

19. _____

20. _____

21. _____

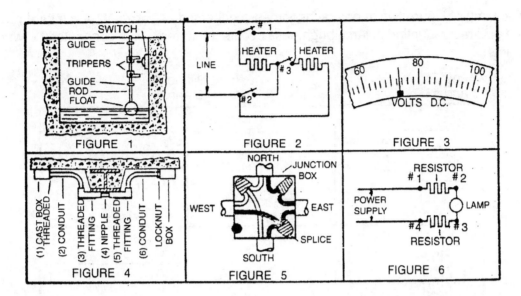

FIGURE 1   FIGURE 2   FIGURE 3

FIGURE 4   FIGURE 5   FIGURE 6

Items 22 - 27.

Items 22 through 27 refer to the figures above. Each item gives the proper figure to use with that item.

22. In Figure 1, the trippers on the float-rod operate the switch and are adjusted to start the pump motor when the water in the sump reaches a certain high level and to stop the pump when the water is down to a certain low level.
If it is decided that the pump should start sooner, the required change in tripper position on the rod is

22.____

     A.   upper tripper lowered   B.   lower tripper lowered
     C.   upper tripper raised   D.   lower tripper raised

23. In Figure 2, the greatest total amount of heat will be provided by the two heaters if

23.____

     A.   switches #2 and #3 are closed
     B.   switch #3 is closed
     C.   switches #1 and #3 are closed
     D.   switches #1, #2 and #3 are closed

24. The voltage indicated on the voltmeter scale of Figure 3 is

24.____

     A.   73.0   B.   71.5   C.   66.5   D.   60.65

25. In Figure 4, if fitting (3) is defective and must be replaced, the proper sequence of disassembly is to remove in the order given

25.____

     A.   2 then 3
     B.   4 then 3
     C.   1, 2 and 3 together; then 3
     D.   6 and 5 together; then 4 and 3

26. If the wiring in the junction box of Figure 5 is in accord with recognized good wiring practice, the power supply wires could NOT be those in the conduit going

26.____

     A.   north   B.   south   C.   east   D.   west

27. The lamp of Figure 6 is at normal brightness connected as shown. Using a third resistor, 27.____
the greatest reduction in lamp brightness occurs if that resistor is connected between
points

   A. #1 and #4   B. #1 and #2
   C. #2 and #3   D. #3 and #4

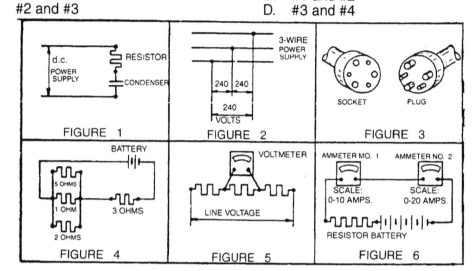

Items 28 - 33.

Items 28 through 33 refer to the figures above. Each item gives the proper figure to use with that
item.

28. In Figure 1, if the voltage of the power supply is constant, the voltage across the con- 28.____
denser is

   A. zero
   B. variable
   C. equal to the supply voltage
   D. more than the supply voltage

29. In accordance with the voltages shown in Figure 2, the power supply must be 29.____

   A. single-phase a.c.   B. two-phase a.c.
   C. three-phase a.c.   D. three-wire d.c.

30. With respect to the plug and socket in Figure 3, it is clear that the plug 30.____

   A. cannot be inserted into the socket
   B. can be inserted into the socket only one way
   C. can be inserted only two ways into the socket
   D. can be inserted three ways into the socket

31. Without knowing the battery voltage in Figure 4, it is clear that the highest current is in 31.____
the

   A. 5-ohm resistor   B. 3-ohm resistor
   C. 2-ohm resistor   D. 1-ohm resistor

32. If the three resistors in Figure 5 are of equal and relatively low resistance, the voltmeter should read   32.____

    A. one-third line voltage
    B. one-half line voltage
    C. two-thirds line voltage
    D. full line voltage

33. If the current in the circuit of Figure 6 is 6 amperes, the ammeters should read   33.____

    A. 4 amp. on meter #1 and 2 amp. on meter #2
    B. 6 amp. on each meter
    C. 2 amp. on meter #1 and 4 amp. on meter #2
    D. 3 amp. on each meter

34. The voltage drop is 24 volts across resistor   34.____

    #1 12-OHMS #2 18-OHMS #3 16-OHMS #4 14-OHMS
    120 VOLTS

    A. #1   B. #2
    C. #3   D. #4

35. If ammeter #2 reads 60 amp., the reading of ammeter #1 should be about   35.____

    A. 4 amp.
    B. 15 amp.
    C. 60 amp.
    D. 900 amp.

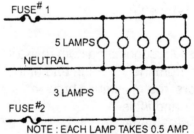

AMMETER #1   AMMETER #2
150 VOLTS   10 VOLTS LOAD
TRANSFORMER

36. If fuse #1 blows in the 3-wire d.c. system shown, the current in the neutral wire will   36.____
    A. increase by 1.0 amp.
    B. increase by 0.5 amp.
    C. decrease by 1.0 amp.
    D. decrease by 0.5 amp.

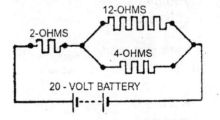

FUSE #1
5 LAMPS
NEUTRAL
3 LAMPS
FUSE #2
NOTE : EACH LAMP TAKES 0.5 AMP.

37. The current in the 4-ohm resistor is   37.____
    A. 5 amp.
    B. 4 amp.
    C. 3 amp.
    D. 1 amp.

12-OHMS
2-OHMS
4-OHMS
20 - VOLT BATTERY

38. On the transformer, the dimension marked "X" is
    A. 9 7/8"
    B. 14"
    C. 18 1/8"
    D. 19 1/8"

38.____

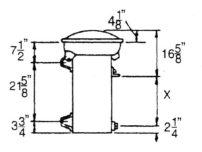

39. With the voltage drop across the four resistors as shown, the voltmeter will read
    A. 50 volts
    B. 70 volts
    C. 100 volts
    D. 170 volts

39.____

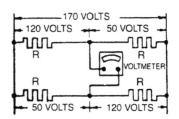

40. If each circuit originates at the switchboard, the total amount of wire required for the conduit runs shown (neglecting connections) is
    A. 5300 ft.
    B. 2650 ft.
    C. 2400 ft.
    D. 1600 ft.

40.____

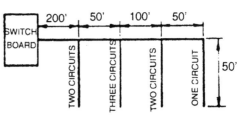

NOTE: TWO WIRES PER CIRCUIT

41. If the permissible current is 1,000 amperes for each square inch of cross section, the bus bar shown can carry
    A. 2250 amp.
    B. 2000 amp.
    C. 1750 amp.
    D. 1500 amp.

41.____

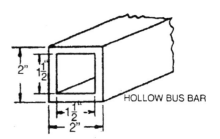

HOLLOW BUS BAR

42. If the slider connecting both resistors is 9 inches from the left-hand end of the resistors, the resistance between terminals #1 and #2 is
    A. 1125 ohms
    B. 875 ohms
    C. 750 ohms
    D. 625 ohms

42.____

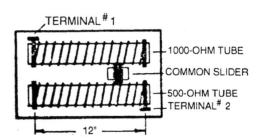

43. If the voltmeter reads 80 volts, the current in the 11-ohm resistor is
    A. 10 amp.
    B. 6.3 amp.
    C. 12 amp.
    D. 8.3 amp.

43.____

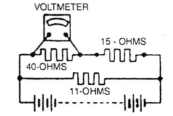

122

Questions 44 - 50.

Questions 44 through 50 show common electrical jobs. Each item shows four methods (A), (B), (C), and (D) of doing the particular job. Only *ONE* of the four methods is entirely *CORRECT* in accordance with good practice. For each item, examine the four sketches and select the sketch showing the correct method. *PRINT,* in the correspondingly numbered item space at the right, the letter given below your selected sketch.

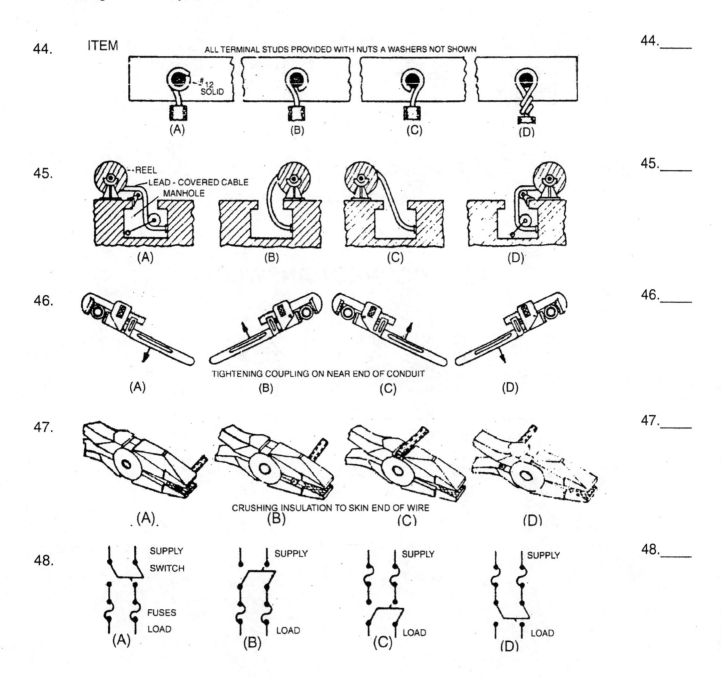

44. ITEM — ALL TERMINAL STUDS PROVIDED WITH NUTS A WASHERS NOT SHOWN — #12 SOLID — (A) (B) (C) (D)

44.____

45. REEL — LEAD - COVERED CABLE — MANHOLE — (A) (B) (C) (D)

45.____

46. TIGHTENING COUPLING ON NEAR END OF CONDUIT — (A) (B) (C) (D)

46.____

47. CRUSHING INSULATION TO SKIN END OF WIRE — (A) (B) (C) (D)

47.____

48. SUPPLY SWITCH FUSES LOAD — (A) (B) (C) (D)

48.____

49.

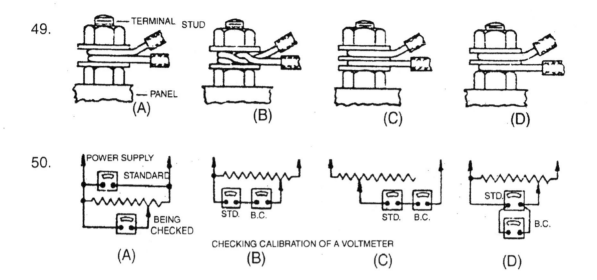

(A)   (B)   (C)   (D)

49.____

50.

(A)   CHECKING CALIBRATION OF A VOLTMETER   (B)   (C)   (D)

50.____

KEY (CORRECT ANSWERS)

1. C	11. A	21. H	31. B	41. C
2. D	12. B	22. D	32. A	42. B
3. C	13. A	23. C	33. B	43. A
4. D	14. C	24. A	34. A	44. B
5. A	15. B	25. D	35. A	45. B
6. B	16. E	26. C	36. B	46. A
7. B	17. D	27. C	37. C	47. D
8. D	18. J	28. C	38. C	48. B
9. D	19. E	29. C	39. B	49. C
10. B	20. K	30. D	40. A	50. D

EXAMINATION SECTION
TEST 1

DIRECTIONS: Each question or incomplete statement is followed by several suggested answers or completions. Select the one that BEST answers the question or completes the statement. *PRINT THE LETTER OF THE CORRECT ANSWER IN THE SPACE AT THE RIGHT.*

1. Motor speeds are *generally* measured directly in RPM by the use of a   1.____

   A.   potentiometer   B.   manometer
   C.   dynamometer   D.   tachometer

2. Asbestos is used as a wire covering *mainly* for protection against   2.____

   A.   humidity   B.   vibration   C.   corrosion   D.   heat

3. Assume that you were asked to get the tools for a maintainer to use in taking down a run   3.____
   of exposed conduit (including outlet boxes) from its installed location on the surface of a
   concrete wall. The combination of tools which would *probably* prove MOST useful would
   be

   A.   Stillson wrenches, a box wrench, and a hacksaw
   B.   hacksaw, a screw driver, and an adjustable open-end wrench
   C.   screw driver, a hammer, and a box wrench
   D.   screw driver, an adjustable open-end wrench, and Stillson wrenches

4. Locknuts are frequently used in making electrical connections on terminal boards.   4.____
   The purpose of the locknuts is to

   A.   eliminate the use of flat washers
   B.   prevent unauthorized personnel from tampering with the connections
   C.   keep the connections from loosening through vibration
   D.   increase the contact area at the connection point

5. The fasteners used to mount a cast iron box on a hollow tile wall are   5.____

   A.   machine screws   B.   lag screws
   C.   toggle bolts   D.   steel cut nails

6. The *primary* purpose of galvanizing steel conduit is to   6.____

   A.   increase mechanical strength
   B.   retard rusting
   C.   provide a good surface for painting
   D.   provide good electrical contact for grounding

7. The BEST immediate first aid if electrolyte splashes into the eyes when filling a storage   7.____
   battery is to

   A.   bandage the eyes to keep out light
   B.   wipe the eyes dry with a soft towel
   C.   induce tears to flow by staring at a bright light
   D.   bathe the eyes with plenty of clean water

8. Transit workers are advised to report injuries caused by nails, no matter how slight. The MOST important reason for this rule is that this type of injury   8.____

    A. is caused by violating safety rules
    B. can only be caused by carelessness
    C. generally causes dangerous bleeding
    D. may result in a serious condition

9. The MOST important reason for using a fuse-puller when removing a cartridge fuse from the fuse clips is to   9.____

    A. prevent blowing of the fuse
    B. prevent injury to the fuse element
    C. reduce the chances of personal injury
    D. reduce arcing at the fuse clips

10. The *three* elements of a transistor are   10.____

    A. collector, base, emitter
    C. plate, grid, emitter
    B. collector, grid, cathode
    D. plate, base, cathode

11. The abbreviation D.P.D.T. used in electrical work describes a type of   11.____

    A. switch   B. motor   C. fuse   D. generator

12. The device used to change a.c. to d.c. is a   12.____

    A. frequency changer
    C. transformer
    B. regulator
    D. rectifier

13. The core of an electro-magnet is *usually* made of   13.____

    A. lead   B. iron   C. brass   D. aluminium

14. The application of lubricating oil to parts of electrical contacts is *generally* considered POOR practice.
The MAIN reason for this is that the   14.____

    A. contacts will slip too much
    B. oil would cause poor electrical contact
    C. oil would reduce the contact resistance
    D. oil would cause a fire

15. Nichrome wire would be MOST suitable for use in   15.____

    A. a transformer
    C. a heating element
    B. a motor
    D. an incandescent lamp

16. To smooth out the ripples present in rectified a.c., the device *commonly* used is a   16.____

    A. filter   B. relay   C. spark gap   D. booster

17. One DISADVANTAGE of porcelain as an insulator is that it is   17.____

    A. only good for low voltage
    B. not satisfactory on a.c. circuits
    C. a brittle material
    D. difficult to clean

18. The gage used to determine the size of wire is called 18.____

    A. AWG   B. NPT   C. PILC   D. RHW

19. A stranded wire is given the same size designation as a solid wire if it has the same 19.____

    A. cross-sectional area   B. weight per foot
    C. overall diameter   D. strength

20. The normal voltage of the electrical circuits in most homes and offices in this area is 120. The *difference* between the maximum power that can be supplied by a 20-ampere circuit and the maximum that can be supplied by a 15-ampere circuit is 20.____

    A. 4200 watts   B. 2400 watts   C. 1800 watts   D. 600 watts

21. The term which is NOT applicable in describing the construction of a microphone is 21.____

    A. dynamic   B. carbon   C. crystal   D. feedback

22. The magnetic material used in making the high-strength permanent magnets which are now readily available, is *commonly* known as 22.____

    A. alnico   B. chromaloy   C. nichrome   D. advance

23. If a two wire circuit has a drop of 2 volts in each wire to the load and a supply voltage of 100 volts, the voltage at the load is _____ volts. 23.____

    A. 104   B. 102   C. 98   D. 96

24. A milliampere is _____ amperes. 24.____

    A. 1000   B. 100   C. .01   D. .001

25. A megohm is _____ ohms. 25.____

    A. 10   B. 100   C. 1000   D. 1,000,000

26. A circular mil is a measure of electrical conductor 26.____

    A. length   B. area   C. volume   D. weight

27. A standard pipe thread differs from a standard screw thread in that the pipe thread 27.____

    A. is tapered
    B. is deeper
    C. requires no lubrication when cutting
    D. has the same pitch for any diameter of pipe

28. The rating term "1000 ohms, 10 watts" would *generally* be applied to a 28.____

    A. heater   B. relay   C. resistor   D. transformer

29. The term "60 cycle" as applied to alternating current means 29.____

    A. one cycle in 60 seconds   B. 60 cycles per second
    C. 60 cycles per minute   D. one cycle in 60 minutes

30. The dimensions of the concrete base shown below are 30.____

    A. 12" x 20"   B. 19" x 25"   C. 21" x 27"   D. 24" x 29"

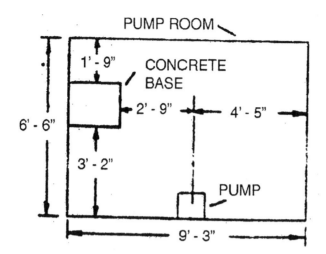

31. Two separate adjacent lamp bulbs are placed behind each colored lens of the train sig-   31.____
    nals alongside the tracks in the subway.
    The *logical* reason why two bulbs are used instead of one bulb is to

    A. permit lower line voltage
    B. increase the light intensity
    C. permit the use of smaller bulbs
    D. keep the signal lighted in case one bulb fails

32. The action of a common plug fuse depends on the principle that the   32.____

    A. current develops heat
    B. voltage breaks down a thin mica disk
    C. current expands and bends a link
    D. voltage develops heat

33. The load side is *usually* wired to the blades of a knife switch to   33.____

    A. prevent arcing when switch is opened
    B. make the blades dead when switch is open
    C. allow changing of fuses without opening switch
    D. prevent blowing fuse when opening switch

34. Two 500-watt lamps connected in series across a 110-volt line draw 2 amperes.   34.____
    The *total* power consumed is _____ watts.

    A. 1,000   B. 250   C. 220   D. 55

35. Before connecting two generators in parallel to a common bus they should ALWAYS   35.____
    have the same

    A. voltage   B. capacity   C. resistance   D. speed

36. Certain electrical control circuits in power stations must be kept energized at all times   36.____
    even in case of complete station shut down.
    Based on this fact, the BEST source of power supply for these circuit is from

    A. the main generator   B. a motor-generator set
    C. a rectifier   D. a storage battery

37. Electrical helpers on the subway system are instructed in the use of fire extinguishers. The *probable* reason for including helpers in this instruction is that the helper

    A. cannot do the more important work
    B. may be the cause of a fire because of his inexperience
    C. may be alone when a fire starts
    D. will become interested in fire prevention

37.____

38. If a 100-watt tungsten lamp is compared with a 25-watt tungsten lamp of the same voltage rating, the resistance of the 100-watt lamp is

    A. higher
    B. lower
    C. the same
    D. higher with A.C., lower with D.C.

38.____

39. If a low resistance is connected in parallel with a higher resistance, the combined resistance is

    A. ALWAYS *less* than the low resistance
    B. ALWAYS *more* than the high resistance
    C. ALWAYS between the values of the high and the low resistance
    D. *higher* or *lower* than the low resistance depending on the value of the higher resistance

39.____

40. Connecting dry cells in parallel instead of in series

    A. *increases* the current capacity of the battery
    B. *decreases* the current capacity of the battery
    C. *increases* the battery voltage
    D. *decreases* the life of the battery

40.____

KEY (CORRECT ANSWERS)

1.	D	11.	A	21.	D	31.	D
2.	D	12.	D	22.	A	32.	A
3.	D	13.	B	23.	D	33.	B
4.	C	14.	B	24.	D	34.	C
5.	C	15.	C	25.	D	35.	A
6.	B	16.	A	26.	B	36.	D
7.	D	17.	C	27.	A	37.	C
8.	D	18.	A	28.	C	38.	B
9.	C	19.	A	29.	B	39.	A
10.	A	20.	D	30.	B	40.	A

TEST 2

1. Maintainers of the transit system are required to report defective equipment to their superiors, even when the maintenance of the particular equipment is handled entirely by another bureau.
The purpose of this rule is to

    A. fix responsibility
    C. encourage alertness
    B. discourage slackers
    D. prevent accidents

1.____

2. To determine which wire of a two-wire 120-volt a.c. line is the underground wire, the BEST procedure is to

    A. obtain the polarity by connecting a voltmeter across the line
    B. quickly ground each line in turn
    C. connect one lead of a test lamp to the conduit; and test with the other
    D. test with the fingers to ground

2.____

3. Condensers are often connected across relay contacts that make and break frequently. The purpose of using condensers in this manner is to

    A. store a charge for the next operation
    B. reduce pitting of the contacts
    C. balance the inductance of the circuit
    D. make the relay slow acting

3.____

4. A conductor used as a ground wire is *usually*

    A. insulated
    C. fused
    B. clamped to the metallic ground
    D. #14 A.W.G.

4.____

5. If fuse clips become hot under normal circuit load, the MOST probable cause is that the fuse

    A. rating is too low
    C. clips are too loose
    B. rating is too high
    D. clips are too tight

5.____

6. The liquid in a lead-acid storage battery is called the

    A. anode
    C. electrolyte
    B. cathode
    D. electrode

6.____

7. In carrying a length of conduit through a reasonably crowded subway station, a maintainer and his helper would follow the BEST procedure if

    A. the helper held one end and the maintainer the other at arm's length downward
    B. the helper carried it near the middle and the maintainer went ahead to warn passengers
    C. each employee carried one end on his shoulder
    D. the two employees carry at the 1/3 and 2/3 points respectively

7.____

8. As a helper you are assigned to work with a maintainer. During the course of the work, you realize that the maintainer is about to violate a basic safety rule.
In this case the BEST thing for you to do is to

    A. walk away from him so that you will not become involved
    B. say nothing until he actually violates this rule and then call it to his attention
    C. immediately call it to his attention
    D. say nothing, but later report this action to the foreman

8.____

9. A rule of the transit system is that the system telephones must NOT be used for personal calls.
The MOST important reason for this rule is that such personal calls

    A. increase telephone maintenance
    B. tie up telephones which may be urgently needed for company business
    C. waste company time
    D. require additional operators

9.____

10. Commutators are found on

    A. mercury rectifiers   B. D.C. motors
    C. circuit breakers   D. alternators

10.____

11. A 200 R.P.M. motor has its centrifugal speed switch set to open at 110% speed.
The switch will open at _____ R.P.M.

    A. 310   B. 220   C. 110   D. 10

11.____

12. A 2-ohm resistor and a 1-ohm resistor connected in parallell2 take a total current of 30 amperes.
The current in the 1-ohm resistor is _____ amperes.

    A. 10   B. 15   C. 20   D. 30

12.____

13. The device *commonly* used to measure the insulation resistance of a transformer winding is

    A. an ammeter   B. a megger
    C. a wattmeter   D. a Wheatstone bridge

13.____

14. A D.C. wattmeter has

    A. a voltage coil and a current coil
    B. two current coils
    C. two voltage coils
    D. three current coils

14.____

15. A 10-24 machine screw necessarily differs from a 12-24 machine screw in

    A. diameter   B. threads per inch
    C. length   D. shape of head

15.____

16. A power transformer with a ratio of 2 to 1 is fully loaded with 1,000 watts on the secondary.
It is reasonable to expect a primary input of _____ watts.

    A. 500   B. 990   C. 1010   D. 2000

16.____

17. The helper who would probably be rated *highest* by his supervisor is the one who   17.____

    A. makes many suggestions on work procedures
    B. never lets the maintainer do heavy lifting
    C. asks many questions about the work
    D. listens to instructions and carries them out

18. A "shunt" is used in parallel with a meter measuring high currents to   18.____

    A. increase the meter resistance
    B. protect the meter against short circuits
    C. reduce the meter current
    D. steady the meter needle

19. A transit employee is required to make a written report of any unusual occurrences promptly.   19.____
The BEST reason for requiring such promptness is that

    A. the report will tend to be more accurate as to facts
    B. the employee will not be as likely to forget to make the report
    C. there is always a tendency to do a better job under pressure
    D. the report may be too long if made at an employee's convenience

20. One thousand volts d.c. is to be tried out on the third-rail of an experimental section of a   20.____
rapid-transit railroad to be built for another city. This voltage is higher than the third-rail
voltage of the New York City subways by about _____ volts.

    A. 100　　　　B. 200　　　　C. 300　　　　D. 400

21. The terminal voltage with batteries connected as shown is _____ volts.   21.____
    A. 0
    B. 1 1/2
    C. 3
    D. 6

TERMINAL VOLTAGE

4 CELLS EACH OF 1 1/2 VOLTS

22. The voltage across terminal 1 and terminal 2 of the transformer connected as shown is _____ volts.   22.____
    A. 50
    B. 100
    C. 200
    D. 400

50 - TURNS　50 - TURNS
100 - TURNS
TERM 1
TERM 2
100 VOLTS

23. The total resistance in the circuit shown between terminal 1 and terminal 2 is _____ ohms.   23.____
    A. 1 1/2
    B. 6
    C. 9
    D. 15

6 - OHMS
5 - OHMS
6 - OHMS
TERM 1
TERM 2

24. The power used by the heater shown is
_____ watts.
   A. 120
   B. 720
   C. 2400
   D. 4320

24.____

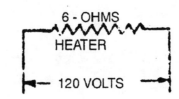

6 - OHMS
HEATER
120 VOLTS

25. The current flowing through the 6-ohm
resistor in the circuit shown is _____
amperes.
   A. 1
   B. 3
   C. 6
   D. 11

25.____

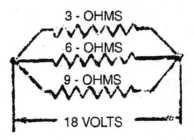

3 - OHMS
6 - OHMS
9 - OHMS
18 VOLTS

26. The voltage across the 30-ohm resistor
in the circuit shown is _____ volts.
   A. 4
   B. 20
   C. 60
   D. 120

26.____

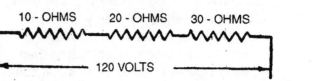

10 - OHMS   20 - OHMS   30 - OHMS
120 VOLTS

27. The current in the wire at the point indicated by the arrow is _____ amperes.

27.____

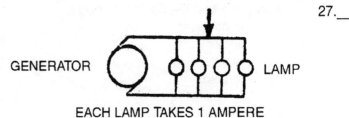

GENERATOR   LAMP
EACH LAMP TAKES 1 AMPERE

28. The sketch shows a head-on view of a
three-pronged plug used with portable
electrical power tools. Considering the
danger of shock when using such tools, it
is evident that the function of the U-
shaped prong is to
   A. insure that the other two prongs
      enter the outlet with the proper
      polarity
   B. provide a half-voltage connection
      when doing light work
   C. prevent accidental pulling of the
      plug from the outlet
   D. connect the metallic shell of the
      tool motor to ground

28.____

29. The reading of the ammeter should be
    A. 4.0
    B. 2.0
    C. 1.0
    D. .05

29.____

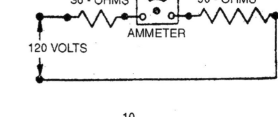

30. Applying your knowledge of electrical measuring instruments, it is *most likely* that the scale shown is for
    A. an ohmmeter
    B. a voltmeter
    C. an ammeter
    D. a wattmeter

30.____

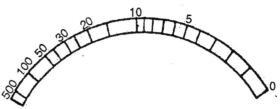

31. Assume that you have decided to test a sealed box having two terminals by using the hook-up shown. When you hold the test prods on the terminals, the voltmeter needle swings upscale and then quickly returns to zero. As an initial conclusion you would be CORRECT in assuming that the box contained a
    A. condenser
    B. choke
    C. rectifier
    D. resistor

31.____

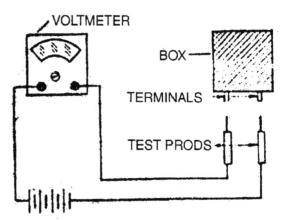

32. If each of the four 90° conduit elbows has the dimensions shown, the distance S is
    A. 20"
    B. 22"
    C. 24"
    D. 26"

32.____

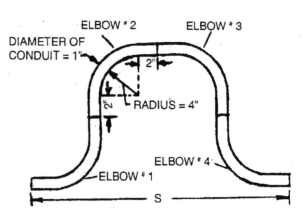

33. The purpose of the auxiliary blade on the knife switch shown is to
   A. delay the opening of the circuit when the handle is pulled open
   B. cut down arcing by opening the circuit quickly
   C. retain the blades in place
   D. increase the capacity of the switch

33.____

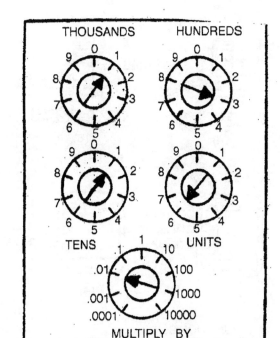

34. The sketch shows the four resistance dials and the multiplying dial of a resistance bridge. The four resistance dials can be set to any value of resistance up to 10,000 ohms, and the multiplier can be set at any of the nine points shown. In their present positions, the five pointers indicate a reading of
   A. 13.60
   B. 136.000
   C. 131.600
   D. 13.16

34.____

35. Regardless of the battery voltage, it is clear that the SMALLEST current is in the resistor having a resistance of
   A. 200 ohms
   B. 300 ohms
   C. 400 ohms
   D. 500 ohms

35.____

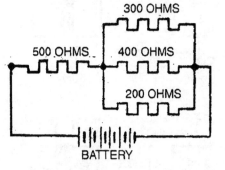

36. The five lamps shown are each rated at 120-volts, 60-watts. If all are good lamps, lamp no. 5 will be
   A. much brighter than normal
   B. about its normal brightness
   C. much dimmer than normal
   D. completely dark

36.____

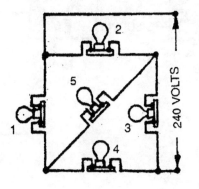

135

QUESTIONS 37-40.

Questions 37-40 inclusive show common electrical maintenance installation jobs. Each question shows four methods (A), (B), (C), and (D) of doing the particular job. Only ONE of the four methods is entirely CORRECT in accordance with good practice. For each question, examine the four sketches and select the sketch showing the correct method. PRINT on your answer sheet, in the correspondingly numbered question space, the letter given below your selected sketch.

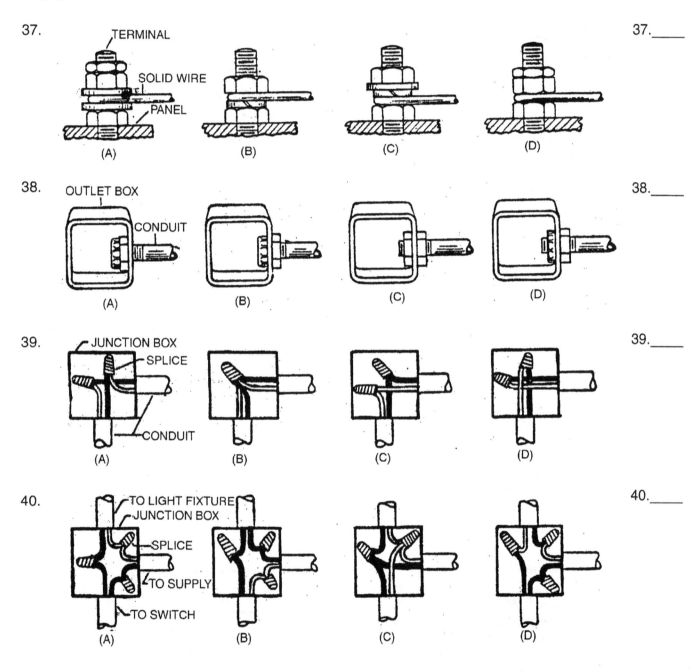

37.   37.____

38.   38.____

39.   39.____

40.   40.____

KEY (CORRECT ANSWERS)

1.	D	11.	B	21.	C	31.	A
2.	C	12.	C	22.	A	32.	D
3.	B	13.	B	23.	B	33.	B
4.	B	14.	A	24.	C	34.	D
5.	C	15.	A	25.	B	35.	C
6.	C	16.	C	26.	C	36.	D
7.	A	17.	D	27.	B	37.	A
8.	C	18.	C	28.	D	38.	B
9.	B	19.	A	29.	C	39.	C
10.	B	20.	D	30.	A	40.	A

———

MECHANICAL APTITUDE

EXAMINATION SECTION
TEST 1

MECHANICAL COMPREHENSION

DIRECTIONS: Questions 1 to 4 test your ability to understand general mechanical devices. Pictures are shown and questions asked about the mechanical devices shown in the picture. Read each question and study the picture. Each question is followed by four choices. For each question, choose the one BEST answer (A, B, C, or D). Then *PRINT THE LETTER OF THE CORRECT ANSWER IN THE SPACE AT THE RIGHT.*

1. The reason for crossing the belt connecting these wheels is to   1.____

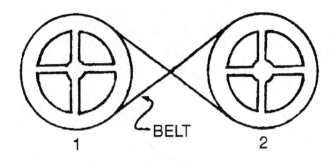

BELT

1   2

    A.   make the wheels turn in opposite directions
    B.   make wheel 2 turn faster than wheel 1
    C.   save wear on the belt
    D.   take up slack in the belt

2. The purpose of the small gear between the two large gears is to   2.____

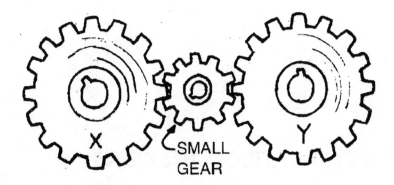

X   SMALL
         GEAR   Y

    A.   increase the speed of the larger gears
    B.   allow the larger gears to turn in different directions
    C.   decrease the speed of the larger gears
    D.   make the larger gears turn in the same direction

3. Each of these three-foot-high water cans have a bottom with an area of-one square foot.   3.____
   The pressure on the bottom of the cans is

 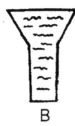 

      A   B   C

A.   least in A   B.   least in B
C.   least in C   D.   the same in all

4. The reading on the scale should be   4.____

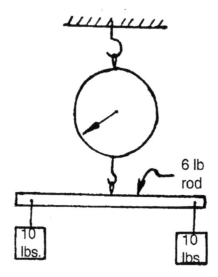

A.   zero
B.   10 pounds
C.   13 pounds
D.   26 pounds

—————

KEY (CORRECT ANSWERS)

1.   A
2.   D
3.   D
4.   D

—————

TEST 2

DIRECTIONS: Questions 1 to 6 test knowledge of tools and how to use them. For each question, decide which one of the four things shown in the boxes labeled A, B, C, or D normally is used with or goes best with the thing in the picture on the left. Then *PRINT THE LETTER OF THE CORRECT ANSWER IN THE SPACE AT THE RIGHT.*

NOTE: All tools are NOT drawn to the same scale.

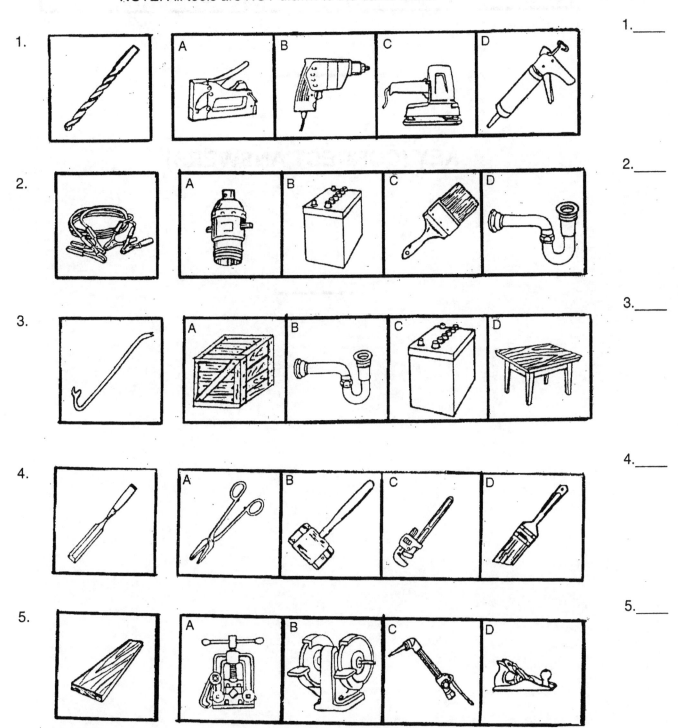

1.____

2.____

3.____

4.____

5.____

6.

A   B   C   D

6.____

_____

KEY (CORRECT ANSWERS)

1.	B	4.	B
2.	B	5.	D
3.	A	6.	B

_____

EXAMINATION SECTION
TEST 1

DIRECTIONS: The questions in this test refer to the use of tools shown below. Read the question, and for the operation given, select the proper tool to be used from those shown. *PRINT* on your answer sheet, in the correspondingly numbered item space, the letter given below your selected tool.

KEY: CORRECT ANSWERS APPEAR AT THE END OF THIS TEST.

1.   Tightening a coupling on the end of a piece of conduit
2.   Making a hole in a concrete wall for a lead anchor
3.   Cutting a one-inch conduit
4.   Loosening the wire connection on the terminal of a standard electric light socket
5.   Cutting 3/0 insulated copper cable
6.   Measuring the total length of several coupled pieces of straight conduit behind a live switchboard without an assistant
7.   Cutting a piece of #10 bare copper wire
8.   Cleaning the burrs from the end of a piece of conduit after cutting
9.   Tightening the drill in the chuck of an electric drill
10.   Tightening the nut on a small stud terminal

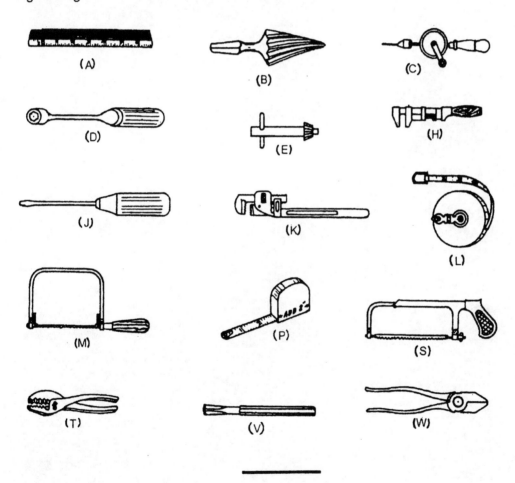

KEY (CORRECT ANSWERS)

1.	K	6.	A
2.	V	7.	W
3.	S	8.	B
4.	J	9.	E
5.	S	10.	D

———

TEST 2

DIRECTIONS: The questions in this test refer to the use of tools shown below. Read the question, and for the operation given, select the proper tool to be used from those shown. *PRINT* on your answer sheet, in the correspondingly numbered item space, the letter given below your selected tool.

KEY : CORRECT ANSWERS APPEAR AT THE END OF THIS TEST.

1. Tightening lag screws which hold a bracket to a wooden post
2. Making holes for sheet metal screws in 20-gauge sheet metal
3. Finishing the surface of a concrete sidewalk
4. Enlarging the hole in a steel strap to take a larger diameter machine screw
5. Installing an elbow fitting on the end of a pipe
6. Making a 3/4" hole in a wooden timber
7. Removing the rough edges from the outside of a pipe after cutting with a hacksaw
8. Cutting out a circular piece from a tin sheet
9. Removing the head from a bolt that is rusted in place
10. Making a hole through a brick wall for the installation of a 1" water pipe

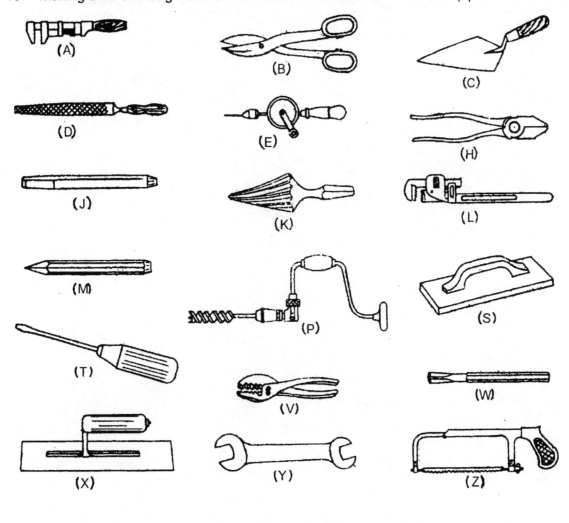

(A)

(B)

(C)

(D)

(E)

(H)

(J)

(K)

(L)

(M)

(P)

(S)

(T)

(V)

(W)

(X)

(Y)

(Z)

KEY (CORRECT ANSWERS)

1. Y
2. E
3. S or X
4. E
5. L

6. P
7. D
8. B
9. J
10. M or W

TEST 3

DIRECTIONS: The questions in this test refer to the use of tools shown below. Read the question, and for the operation given, select the proper tool to be used from those shown. *PRINT* on your answer sheet, in the correspondingly numbered item space, the letter given below your selected tool.

KEY: CORRECT ANSWERS APPEAR AT THE END OF THIS TEST.

1. Lifting a track rail to insert a steel plate between tie and rail
2. Drilling a shallow one-inch diameter hole in the concrete roadbed
3. Cutting a piece from a 2" diameter steel rod
4. Center-punching a steel plate before drilling a hole
5. Checking the two rails of a track for level
6. Tightening hexagon head screw spikes into a track tie
7. Lining up holes in two heavy metal plates before inserting a bolt
8. Making a half-twist in a 1/8" x 3/4" iron strap held in a vise
9. Measuring the exact length of rail for a space approximately 30' long
10. Removing a bolt rusted in place by knocking off the nut or head
11. Cutting a shallow groove across a wooden tie

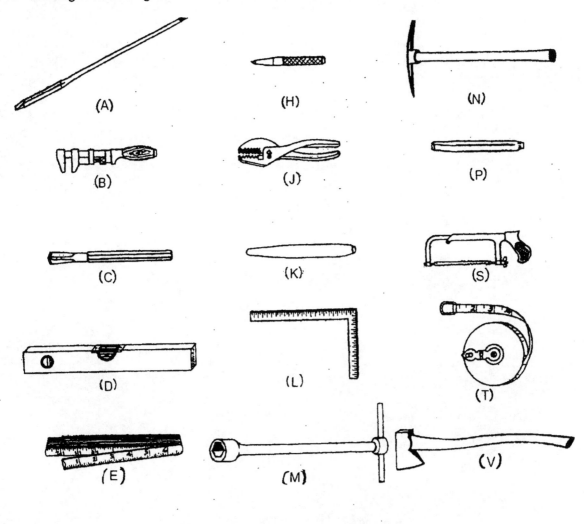

(A)   (H)   (N)

(B)   (J)   (P)

(C)   (K)   (S)

(D)   (L)   (T)

(E)   (M)   (V)

KEY (CORRECT ANSWERS)

1. A
2. C
3. S
4. H
5. D

6. M
7. K
8. B
9. T
10. P

11. V

ARITHMETIC

EXAMINATION SECTION
TEST 1

DIRECTIONS: Each question or incomplete statement is followed by several suggested answers or completions. Select the one that BEST answers the question or completes the statement. *PRINT THE LETTER OF THE CORRECT ANSWER IN THE SPACE AT THE RIGHT.*

1. From 30983 subtract 29998. The answer should be   1.____
    A.   985   B.   995   C.   1005   D.   1015

2. From $2537.75 subtract $1764.28. The answer should be   2.____
    A. $763.58   B. $773.47   C. $774.48   D. $873.58

3. From 254211 subtract 76348. The answer should be   3.____
    A.   177863   B.   177963   C.   187963   D.   188973

4. Divide 4025 by 35. The answer should be   4.____
    A.   105   B.   109   C.   115   D.   125

5. Multiply 0.35 by 2764. The answer should be   5.____
    A.   997.50   B.   967.40   C.   957.40   D.   834.40

6. Multiply 1367 by 0.50. The answer should be   6.____
    A.   6.8350   B.   68.350   C.   683.50   D.   6835.0

7. Multiply 841 by 0.01. The answer should be   7.____
    A.   0.841   B.   8.41   C.   84.1   D.   841

8. Multiply 1962 by 25. The answer should be   8.____
    A.   47740   B.   48460   C.   48950   D.   49050

9. Multiply 905 by 0.05. The answer should be   9.____
    A.   452.5   B.   45.25   C.   4.525   D.   0.4525

10. Multiply 8.93 by 4.7. The answer should be   10.____
    A.   41.971   B.   40.871   C.   4.1971   D.   4.0871

11. Multiply 25 by 763. The answer should be   11.____
    A.   18075   B.   18875   C.   19075   D.   20965

12. Multiply 2530 by 0.10. The answer should be   12.____
    A.   2.5300   B.   25.300   C.   253.00   D.   2530.0

13. Multiply 3053 by 0.25. The answer should be
    A. 76.325   B. 86.315   C. 763.25   D. 863.15

13._____

14. Multiply 6204 by 0.35. The answer should be
    A. 2282.40   B. 2171.40   C. 228.24   D. 217.14

14._____

15. Multiply $.35 by 7619. The answer should be
    A. $2324.75   B. $2565.65   C. $2666.65   D. $2756.75

15._____

16. Multiply 6513 by 45. The answer should be
    A. 293185   B. 293085   C. 292185   D. 270975

16._____

17. Multiply 3579 by 70. The answer should be
    A. 25053.0   B. 240530   C. 250530   D. 259530

17._____

18. A class had an average of 24 words correct on a spelling test. The class average on this spelling test was 80%.
The AVERAGE number of words missed on this test was
    A. 2   B. 4   C. 6   D. 8

18._____

19. In which one of the following is 24 renamed as a product of primes?
    A. 2 x 6 x 2   B. 8 x 3 x 1
    C. 2 x 2 x 3 x 2   D. 3 x 4 x 2

19._____

Questions 20-23.

DIRECTIONS: In answering Questions 20 through 23, perform the indicated operation. Select the BEST answer from the choices below.

20. Add: 7068
            2807
            9434
            <u>6179</u>
    A. 26,488   B. 24,588   C. 25,488   D. 25,478

20._____

21. Divide: $75\sqrt{45555}$
    A. 674   B. 607.4   C. 6074   D. 60.74

21._____

22. Multiply: 907
             <u>x806</u>
    A. 73,142   B. 13,202   C. 721,042   D. 731,042

22._____

23. Subtract: 60085
              <u>-47194</u>
    A. 12,891   B. 13,891   C. 12,991   D. 12,871

23._____

24. A librarian reported that 1/5% of all books taken out last school year had not been returned.
    If 85,000 books were borrowed from the library, how many were not returned?

    A. 170   B. 425   C. 1,700   D. 4,250

    24.____

25. At 40 miles per hour, how many minutes would it take to travel 12 miles?

    A. 30   B. 18   C. 15   D. 20

    25.____

KEY (CORRECT ANSWERS)

1.	A	11.	C
2.	B	12.	C
3.	A	13.	C
4.	C	14.	B
5.	B	15.	C
6.	C	16.	B
7.	B	17.	C
8.	D	18.	C
9.	B	19.	C
10.	A	20.	C

21.	B
22.	D
23.	A
24.	A
25.	B

SOLUTIONS TO PROBLEMS

1. 30,983 - 29,998 = 985

2. $2537.75 - $1764.28 = $773.47

3. 254,211 - 76,348 = 177,863

4. 4025 ÷ 35 = 115

5. (.35)(2764) = 967.4

6. (1367)(.50) = 683.5

7. (841)(.01) = 8.41

8. (1962)(25) = 49,050

9. (905)(.05) = 45.25

10. (8.93)(4.7) = 41.971

11. (25)(763) = 19,075

12. (2530)(.10) = 253

13. (3053)(.25) = 763.25

14. (6204)(.35) = 2171.4

15. ($.35)(7619) = $2666.65

16. (6513)(45) = 293,085

17. (3579)(70) = 250,530

18. 24 ÷ .80 = 30. Then, 30 - 24 = 6 words

19. 24 = 2 x 2 x 3 x 2, where each number is a prime.

20. 7068 ÷ 2807 + 9434 + 6179 = 25,488

21. 45,555 ÷ 75 = 607.4

22. (907)(806) = 731,042

23. 60,085 - 47,194 = 12,891

24. (1/5%)(85,000) = (.002)(85,000) = 170 books

25. Let x = number of minutes. Then, $\frac{40}{60} = \frac{12}{x}$. Solving, x = 18

TEST 2

1. The sum of 57901 + 34762 is   1.____
    A. 81663   B. 82663   C. 91663   D. 92663

2. The sum of 559 + 448 + 362 + 662 is   2.____
    A. 2121   B. 2031   C. 2021   D. 1931

3. The sum of 36153 + 28624 + 81379 is   3.____
    A. 136156   B. 146046   C. 146146   D. 146156

4. The sum of 742 + 9197 + 8972 is   4.____
    A. 19901   B. 18911   C. 18801   D. 17921

5. The sum of 7989 + 8759 + 2726 is   5.____
    A. 18455   B. 18475   C. 19464   D. 19474

6. The sum of $111.55 + $95.05 + $38.80 is   6.____
    A. $234.40   B. $235.30   C. $245.40   D. $254.50

7. The sum of 1302 + 46187 + 92610 + 4522 is   7.____
    A. 144621   B. 143511   C. 134621   D. 134521

8. The sum of 47953 + 58041 + 63022 + 22333 is   8.____
    A. 170248   B. 181349   C. 191349   D. 200359

9. The sum of 76563 + 43693 + 38521 + 50987 + 72723 is   9.____
    A. 271378   B. 282386   C. 282487   D. 292597

10. The sum of 85923 + 97211 + 11333 + 4412 + 22533 is   10.____
    A. 209302   B. 212422   C. 221412   D. 221533

11. The sum of 4299 + 54163 + 89765 + 1012 + 38962 is   11.____
    A. 188201   B. 188300   C. 188301   D. 189311

12. The sum of 48526 + 709 + 11534 + 80432 + 6096 is   12.____
    A. 135177   B. 139297   C. 147297   D. 149197

13. The sum of $407.62 + $109.01 + $68.44 + $378.68 is   13.____
    A. $963.75   B. $964.85   C. $973.65   D. $974.85

14. From 40614 subtract 4697. The answer should be

    A.   35917   B.   35927   C.   36023   D.   36027

14._____

15. From 81773 subtract 5717. The answer should be

    A.   75964   B.   76056   C.   76066   D.   76956

15._____

16. From $1755.35 subtract $1201.75. The answer should be

    A. $542.50   B. $544.50   C. $553.60   D. $554.60

16._____

17. From $2402.10 subtract $998.85. The answer should be

    A. $1514.35   B. $1504.25   C. $1413.25   D. $1403.25

17._____

18. Add: 12 1/2
               2 1/2
               <u>3 1/2</u>

    A.   17   B.   17 1/4   C.   17 3/4   D.   18

18._____

19. Subtract: 150
                   <u>-80</u>

    A.   70   B.   80   C.   130   D.   150

19._____

20. After cleaning up some lots in the city dump, five cleanup crews loaded the following amounts of garbage on trucks:

        Crew No. 1 loaded 2 1/4 tons
        Crew No. 2 loaded 3 tons
        Crew No. 3 loaded 1 1/4 tons
        Crew No. 4 loaded 2 1/4 tons
        Crew No. 5 loaded 1/2 ton.

The TOTAL number of tons of garbage loaded was

    A.   8 1/4   B.   8 3/4   C.   9   D.   9 1/4

20._____

21. Subtract: 17 3/4
                <u>-7 1/4</u>

    A.   7 1/2   B.   10 1/2   C.   14 1/4   D.   17 3/4

21._____

22. Yesterday, Tom and Bill each received 10 leaflets about rat control. They were supposed to distribute one leaflet to each supermarket in the neighborhood. When the day was over, Tom had 8 leaflets left. Bill had no leaflets left.
How many supermarkets got leaflets yesterday?

    A.   8   B.   10   C.   12   D.   18

22._____

23. What is 2/3 of 1 1/8?

    A.   1 11/16   B.   3/4   C.   3/8   D.   4 1/3

23._____

24. A farmer bought a load of 120 bushels of corn.
After he fed 45 bushels to his hogs, what fraction of his supply remained?

    A.   5/8   B.   3/5   C.   3/8   D.   4/7

24._____

25. In the numeral 3,159,217, the 2 is in the _____ column.   25._____

    A. hundreds   B. units   C. thousands   D. tens

———

KEY (CORRECT ANSWERS)

1.	D		11.	A
2.	B		12.	C
3.	D		13.	A
4.	B		14.	A
5.	D		15.	B
6.	C		16.	C
7.	A		17.	D
8.	C		18.	D
9.	C		19.	A
10.	C		20.	D

21. B
22. C
23. B
24. A
25. A

———

SOLUTIONS TO PROBLEMS

1. $57,901 + 34,762 = 92,663$

2. $559 + 448 + 362 + 662 = 2031$

3. $36,153 + 28,624 + 81,379 = 146,156$

4. $742 + 9197 + 8972 = 18,911$

5. $7989 + 8759 + 2726 = 19,474$

6. $\$111.55 + \$95.05 + \$38.80 = \$245.40$

7. $1302 + 46,187 + 92,610 + 4522 = 144,621$

8. $47,953 + 58,041 + 63,022 + 22,333 = 191,349$

9. $76,563 + 45,693 + 38,521 + 50,987 + 72,723 = 282,487$

10. $85,923 + 97,211 + 11,333 + 4412 + 22,533 = 221,412$

11. $4299 + 54,163 + 89,765 + 1012 + 38,962 = 188,201$

12. $48,526 + 709 + 11,534 + 80,432 + 6096 = 147,297$

13. $\$407.62 + \$109.01 + \$68.44 + \$378.68 = \$963.75$

14. $40,614 - 4697 = 35,917$

15. $81,773 - 5717 = 76,056$

16. $\$1755.35 - \$1201.75 = \$553.60$

17. $\$2402.10 - \$998.85 = \$1403.25$

18. $12\ 1/2 + 2\ 1/4 + 3\ 1/4 = 17\ 4/4 = 18$

19. $150 - 80 = 70$

20. $2\ 1/4 + 3 + 1\ 1/4 + 2\ 1/4 + 1/2 = 8\ 5/4 = 9\ 1/4$ tons

21. $17\ 3/4 - 7\ 1/4 = 10\ 2/4 = 10\ 1/2$

22. $10 + 10 - 8 - 0 = 12$ supermarkets

23. $\left(\frac{2}{3}\right)\left(1\frac{1}{8}\right) = \left(\frac{2}{3}\right)\left(\frac{9}{8}\right) = \frac{18}{24} = \frac{3}{4}$

24. $120 - 45 = 75$. Then, $\frac{75}{120} = \frac{5}{8}$

25. The number 2 is in the hundreds column of 3,159,217

TEST 3

DIRECTIONS: Each question or incomplete statement is followed by several suggested answers or completions. Select the one that BEST answers the question or completes the statement. *PRINT THE LETTER OF THE CORRECT ANSWER IN THE SPACE AT THE RIGHT.*

1. The distance covered in three minutes by a subway train traveling at 30 mph is _____ mile(s).

    A. 3   B. 2   C. 1 1/2   D. 1   1._____

2. A crate contains 3 pieces of equipment weighing 73, 84, and 47 pounds, respectively. The empty crate weighs 16 pounds.
If the crate is lifted by 4 trackmen, each trackman lifting one corner of the crate, the AVERAGE number of pounds lifted by each of the trackmen is   2._____

    A. 68   B. 61   C. 55   D. 51

3. The weight per foot of a length of square-bar 4" x 4" in cross-section, as compared with one 2" x 2" in cross-section, is _____ as much.   3._____

    A. twice   B. 2 1/2 times
    C. 3 times   D. 4 times

4. An order for 360 feet of 2" x 8" lumber is shipped in 20-foot lengths.
The MAXIMUM number of 9-foot pieces that can be cut from this shipment is   4._____

    A. 54   B. 40   C. 36   D. 18

5. If a trackman gets $10.40 per hour and time and one-half for working over 40 hours, his gross salary for a week in which he worked 44 hours should be   5._____

    A. $457.60   B. $478.40   C. $499.20   D. $514.80

6. If a section of ballast 6'-0" wide, 8'-0" long, and 2'-6" deep is excavated, the amount of ballast removed is _____ cu. feet.   6._____

    A. 96   B. 104   C. 120   D. 144

7. The sum of 7'2 3/4", 0'-2 7/8", 3'-0", 4'-6 3/8", and 1'-9 1/4" is   7._____

    A. 16'-8 1/4"   B. 16'-8 3/4"   C. 16'-9 1/4"   D. 16' -9 3/4"

8. The sum of 3 1/16", 4 1/4", 2 5/8", and 5 7/16" is   8._____

    A. 15 3/16"   B. 15 1/4"   C. 15 3/8"   D. 15 1/2"

9. Add: $51.79, $29.39, and $8.98.
The CORRECT answer is   9._____

    A. $78.97   B. $88.96   C. $89.06   D. $90.16

10. Add: $72.07 and $31.54. Then subtract $25.75.
The CORRECT answer is   10._____

    A. $77.86   B. $82.14   C. $88.96   D. $129.36

11. Start with $82.47. Then subtract $25.50, $4.75, and 35¢.
The CORRECT answer is   11.____

    A. $30.60   B. $51.87   C. $52.22   D. $65.25

12. Add: $19.35 and $37.75. Then subtract $9.90 and $19.80.
The CORRECT answer is   12.____

    A. $27.40   B. $37.00   C. $37.30   D. $47.20

13. Add: $153   13.____
            114
            210
        +186

    A. $657   B. $663   C. $713   D. $757

14. Add: $64.91   14.____
          13.53
          19.27
          20.00
       +72.84

    A. $170.25   B. $178.35   C. $180.45   D. $190.55

15. Add: 1963   15.____
         1742
       +2497

    A. 6202   B. 6022   C. 5212   D. 5102

16. Add: 206   16.____
         709
      1342
     +2076

    A. 3432   B. 3443   C. 4312   D. 4333

17. Subtract: $190.76   17.____
         -   .99

    A. $189.97   B. $189.87   C. $189.77   D. $189.67

18. From 99876 subtract 85397. The answer should be   18.____
    A. 14589   B. 14521   C. 14479   D. 13589

19. From $876.51 subtract $92.89. The answer should be   19.____
    A. $773.52   B. $774.72   C. $783.62   D. $784.72

20. From 70935 subtract 49489. The answer should be   20.____
    A. 20436   B. 21446   C. 21536   D. 21546

21. From $391.55 subtract $273.45. The answer should be   21._____

    A. $118.10   B. $128.20   C. $178.10   D. $218.20

22. When 119 is subtracted from the sum of 2016 + 1634, the answer is   22._____

    A. 2460   B. 3531   C. 3650   D. 3769

23. Multiply 35 x 65 x 15. The answer should be   23._____

    A. 2275   B. 24265   C. 31145   D. 34125

24. Multiply: 4.06   24._____
           x.031

    A. 1.2586   B. .12586   C. .02586   D. .1786

25. When 65 is added to the result of 14 multiplied by 13, the answer is   25._____

    A. 92   B. 182   C. 247   D. 16055

KEY (CORRECT ANSWERS)

1.	C	11.	B
2.	C	12.	A
3.	D	13.	B
4.	C	14.	D
5.	B	15.	A
6.	C	16.	D
7.	C	17.	C
8.	C	18.	C
9.	D	19.	C
10.	A	20.	B

21.	A
22.	B
23.	D
24.	B
25.	C

SOLUTIONS TO PROBLEMS

1. Let x = distance. Then, $\dfrac{30}{60} = \dfrac{x}{3}$ Solving, x = 1 1/2 miles

2. (73 + 84 + 47 + 16) ÷ 4 = 55 pounds

3. (4 x 4) ÷ (2 x 2) = a ratio of 4 to 1.

4. 20 ÷ 9 = 2 2/9 , rounded down to 2 pieces. Then, (360 ÷ 20)(2) = 36

5. Salary =($10.40)(40) + ($15.60)(4) = $478.40

6. (6)(8)(2 1/2) = 120 cu.ft.

7. $7'2\dfrac{3}{4}"+0'2\dfrac{7}{8}"+3'0"+4'6\dfrac{3}{8}"+1'9\dfrac{1}{4}"=15'19\dfrac{18}{8}"=15'21\dfrac{1}{4}"=16'9\dfrac{1}{4}"$

8. $3\dfrac{1}{16}"+4\dfrac{1}{4}"+2\dfrac{5}{8}"+5\dfrac{7}{16}"=14\dfrac{22}{16}"=15\dfrac{3}{8}"$

9. $51.79 + $29.39 + $8.98 = $90.16

10. $72.07 + $31.54 = $103.61. Then, $103.61 - $25.75 = $77.86

11. $82.47 - $25.50 - $4.75 - $0.35 = $51.87

12. $19.35 + $37.75 = $57.10. Then, $57.10 - $9.90 - $19.80 = $27.40

13. $153 + $114 + $210 + $186 = $663

14. $64.91 + $13.53 + $19.27 + $20.00 + $72.84 = $190.55

15. 1963 + 1742 + 2497 = 6202

16. 206 + 709 + 1342 + 2076 = 4333

17. $190.76 - .99 = $189.77

18. 99,876 - 85,397 = 14,479

19. $876.51 - $92.89 = $783.62

20. 70,935 - 49,489 = 21,446

21. $391.55 - $273.45 = $118.10

22. (2016 + 1634) - 119 = 3650 - 119 = 3531

23. $(35)(65)(15) = 34,125$

24. $(4.06)(.031) = .12586$

25. $65 + (14)(13) = 65 + 182 = 247$

———

BASIC ELECTRICITY

FUNDAMENTAL CONCEPTS OF ELECTRICITY
What is Electricity?

The word "electric" is actually a Greek-derived word meaning AMBER. Amber is a translucent (semitransparent) yellowish mineral, which, in the natural form, is composed of fossilized resin. The ancient Greeks used the words "electric force" in referring to the mysterious forces of attraction and repulsion exhibited by amber when it was rubbed with a cloth. They did not understand the fundamental nature of this force. They could not answer the seemingly simple question, "What is electricity?". This question is still unanswered. Though you might define electricity as "that force which moves electrons," this would be the same as defining an engine as "that force which moves an automobile." You would have described the effect, not the force.

We presently know little more than the ancient Greeks knew about the fundamental nature of electricity, but tremendous strides have been made in harnessing and using it. Elaborate theories concerning the nature and behavior of electricity have been advanced, and have gained wide acceptance because of their apparent truth and demonstrated workability.

From time to time various scientists have found that electricity seems to behave in a constant and predictable manner in given situations, or when subjected to given conditions. These scientists, such as Faraday, Ohm, Lenz, and Kirchhoff, to name only a few, observed and described the predictable characteristics of electricity and electric current in the form of certain rules. These rules are often referred to as "laws." Thus, though electricity itself has never been clearly defined, its predictable nature and easily used form of energy has made it one of the most widely used power sources in modern time. By learning the rules, or laws, applying to the behavior of electricity, and by learning the methods of producing, controlling, and using it, you will have "learned" electricity without ever having determined its fundamental identity.

THE MOLECULE

One of the oldest, and probably the most generally accepted, theories concerning electric current flow is that it is comprised of moving electrons. This is the ELECTRON THEORY. Electrons are extremely tiny parts, or particles, of matter. To study the electron, you must therefore study the structural nature of matter itself. (Anything having mass and inertia, and which occupies any amount of space, is composed of matter.) To study the fundamental structure or composition of any type of matter, it must be reduced to its fundamental fractions. Assume the drop of water in figure 1-1 (A) was halved again and again. By continuing the process long enough, you would eventually obtain the smallest particle of water possible-the molecule. All molecules are composed of atoms.

A molecule of water (H_2O) is composed of one atom of oxygen and two atoms of hydrogen, as represented in figure 1-1 (B). If the molecule of water were further subdivided, there would remain only unrelated atoms of oxygen and hydrogen, and the water would no longer exist as such. This example illustrates the following fact-the molecule is the smallest particle to which a substance can be reduced and still be called by the same name. This applies to all substances-liquids, solids, and gases.

When whole molecules are combined or separated from one another, the change is generally referred to as a PHYSICAL change. In a CHEMICAL change the molecules of the substance are altered such that

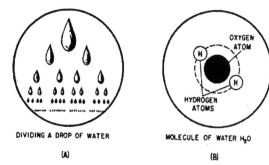

Figure 1-1.—Matter is made up of molecules.

new molecules result. Most chemical changes Involve positive and negative ions and thus are electrical in nature. All matter is said to be essentially electrical in nature.

THE ATOM

In the study of chemistry it soon becomes apparent that the molecule is far from being the ultimate particle into which matter may be subdivided. The salt molecule may be decomposed into radically different substancessodium and chlorine. These particles that make up molecules can be isolated and studied separately. They are called ATOMS.

The atom is the smallest particle that makes up that type of material called an ELEMENT. The element retains its characteristics when subdivided into atoms. More than 100 elements have been identified. They can be arranged into a table of increasing weight, and can be grouped into families of material having similar properties. This arrangement is called the PERIODIC TABLE OF THE ELEMENTS.

The idea that all matter is composed of atoms dates back more than 2,000 years to the Greeks. Many centuries passedbefore the study of matter proved that the basic idea of atomic structure was correct. Physicists have explored the interior of the atom and discovered many subdivisions in it. The core of the atom is called the NUCLEUS. Most of the mass of the atom is concentrated in the nucleus. It is comparable to the sun in the solar system, around which the planets revolve. The nucleus contains PROTONS (positively charged particles) and NEUTRONS which are electrically neutral.

Most of the weight of the atom is in the protons and neutrons of the nucleus. Whirling around the nucleus are one or more smaller particles of negative electric charge. THESE ARE THE ELECTRONS. Normally there is one proton for each electron in the entire atom so that the net positive charge of the nucleus is balanced by the net negative charge of the electrons whirling around the nucleus. THUS THE ATOM IS ELECTRICALLY NEUTRAL.

The electrons do not fall into the nucleus even though they are attracted strongly to it. Their motion prevents it, as the planets are prevented from falling into the sun because of their centrifugal force of revolution.

The number of protons, which is usually the same as the number of electrons, determines the kind of element in question. Figure 1-2 shows a simplified picture of several atoms of different materials based on the conception of planetary electrons describing orbits about the nucleus. For example, hydrogen has a nucleus consisting of 1 proton, around which rotates 1 electron. The helium atom has a nucleus containing 2 protons and 2 neutrons with 2 electrons encircling the nucleus. Near the other extreme of the list of elements is curium (not shown in the figure), an element discovered in the 1940's, which has 96 protons and 96 electrons in each atom.

The *Periodic Table of the Elements* is an orderly arrangement of the elements in ascending atomic number (number of planetary electrons) and also in atomic weight (number of protons and neutrons in the nucleus). The various kinds of atoms have distinct masses or

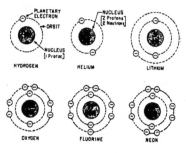

Figure 1-2.—Atomic structure of elements.

weights with respect to each other. The element most closely approaching unity (meaning 1) is hydrogen whose atomic weight is 1.008 as compared with oxygen whose atomic weight is 16. Helium has an atomic weight of approximately 4, lithium 7, fluorine 19, and neon 20, as shown in figure 1-2.

Figure 1-3 is a pictorial summation of the discussion that has just been presented. Visible matter, at the left of the figure, is broken down first to one of its basic molecules, then to one of the molecule's atoms. The atom is then further reduced to its subatomic particlesthe protons, neutrons, and electrons. Subatomic particles are electric in nature. That is, they are the particles of matter most affected by an electric force. Whereas the whole molecule or a whole atom is electrically neutral, most subatomic particles are not neutral (with the exception of the neutron). Protons are inherently positive, and electrons are inherently negative. It is these inherent characteristics which make subatomic particles sensitive to electric force.

When an electric force is applied to a conducting medium, such as copper wire, electrons in the outer orbits of the copper atoms are forced out of orbit and impelled along the wire. The direction of electron movement is determined by the direction of the impelling force. The protons do not move, mainly because they are extremely heavy. The proton of the lightest element, hydrogen, is approximately 1,850 times as heavy as an electron. Thus, it is the relatively light electron that is most readily moved by electricity.

When an orbital electron is removed from an atom it is called a FREE ELECTRON. Some of the electrons of certain metallic atoms are so loosely bound to the nucleus that they are comparatively free to move from atom to atom. Thus, a very small force or amount of energy will cause such electrons to be removed from the atom and become free electrons. It is these free electrons that constitute the flow of an electric current in electrical conductors.

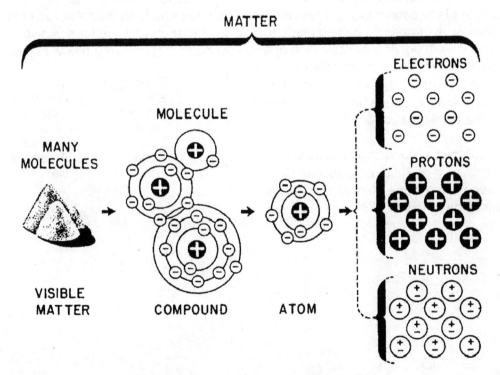

Figure 1-3.—Breakdown of visible matter to electric particles.

If the internal energy of an atom is raised above its normal state, the atom is said to be EXCITED. Excitation may be produced by causing the atoms to collide with particles that are impelled by an electric force. In this way, energy is transferred from the electric source to the atom. The excess energy absorbed by an atom may become sufficient to cause loosely bound outer electrons to leave the atom against the force that acts to hold them within. An atom that has thus lost or gained one or more electrons is said to be IONIZED. If the atom loses electrons it becomes positively charged and is referred to as a POSITIVE ION. Conversely, if the atom gains electrons, it becomes negatively charged and is referred to as a NEGATIVE ION. Actually then, an ion is a small particle of matter having a positive or negative charge.

Conductors and Insulators

Substances that permit the free motion of a large number of electrons are called CONDUCTORS. Copper wire is considered a good conductor because it has many free electrons. Electrical energy is transferred through conductors by means of the movement of free electrons that migrate from atom to atom inside the conductor. Each electron moves a very short distance to the neighboring atom where it replaces one or more electrons by forcing them out of their orbits. The replaced electrons repeat the process in other nearby atoms until the movement is transmitted throughout the entire length of the conductor. The greater the number of electrons that can be made to move in a material under the application of a given force the better are the conductive qualities of that material. A good conductor is said to have a low opposition or low resistance to the current (electron) flow.

In contrast to good conductors, some substances such as rubber, glass, and dry wood have very few free electrons. In these materials large amounts of energy must be expended in order to break the electrons loose from the influence of the nucleus. Substances containing very few free electrons are called POOR CONDUCTORS, NONCONDUCTORS, or INSULATORS. Actually, there is no sharp dividing line between conductors and insulators, since electron motion is known to exist to some extent in all matter. Electricians simply use the best conductors as wires to carry current and the poorest conductors as insulators to prevent the current from being diverted from the wires.

Listed below are some of the best conductors and best insulators arranged in accordance with their respective abilities to conduct or to resist the flow of electrons.

Conductors	Insulators
Silver	Dry air
Copper	Glass
Aluminum	Mica
Zinc	Rubber
Brass	Asbestos
Iron	Bakelite

Static Electricity

In a natural, or neutral state, each atom in a body of matter will have the proper number of electrons in orbit around it. Consequently, the whole body of matter comprised of the neutral atoms will also be electrically neutral. In this state, it is said to have a "zero charge," and will neither attract nor repel other matter in its vicinity. Electrons will neither leave nor enter the neutrally charged body should it come in contact with other neutral bodies. If, however, any number of electrons are removed from the atoms of a body of matter, there will remain more protons than electrons, and the whole body of matter will become electrically positive. Should the positively charged body come in contact with another body having a normal charge, or having a negative (too many electrons) charge, an electric current will flow between them. Electrons will leave the more negative body and enter the positive body. This electron flow will continue until both bodies have equal charges.

When two bodies of matter have unequal charges, and are near one another, an electric force is exerted between them because of their unequal charges. However, since they are not in contact, their charges cannot equalize. The existence of such an electric force, where current cannot flow, is referred to as static electricity. "Static" means "not moving." This is also referred to as an ELECTROSTATIC FORCE.

One of the easiest ways to create a static charge is by the friction method. With the friction method, two pieces of matter are rubbed together and electrons are "wiped off" one onto the other. If materials that are good conductors are used, it is quite difficult to obtain a detectable charge on either. The reason for this is that equalizing currents will flow easily in and between the conducting materials. These currents equalize the charges almost as fast as they are created. A static charge is easier to obtain by rubbing a hard nonconducting material against a soft, or fluffy, nonconductor. Electrons are rubbed off one material and onto the other material. This is illustrated in figure 1-4.

When the hard rubber rod is rubbed in the fur, the rod accumulates electrons. Since both fur and rubber are poor conductors, little equalizing current can flow, and an electrostatic charge is built up. When the charge is great enough, equalizing currents will flow in spite of the material's poor conductivity. These currents will cause visible sparks, if viewed in darkness, and will produce a crackling sound.

CHARGED BODIES

One of the fundamental laws of electricity is that LIKE CHARGES REPEL EACH OTHER and UNLIKE CHARGES ATTRACT EACH OTHER. A positive charge and negative charge, being unlike, tend to move toward each other. In the atom the negative electrons are drawn toward the positive protons in the nucleus. This attractive force is balanced by the electron's centrifugal force caused by its rotation about the nucleus. As a result, the electrons remain in orbit and are not drawn into the nucleus. Electrons repel each other because of their like negative charges, and protons repel each other because of their like positive charges.

The law of charged bodies may be demonstrated by a simple experiment. Two pith (paper pulp) balls are suspended near one another by threads, as shown in figure 1-5.

If the hard rubber rod is rubbed to give it a negative charge, and then held against the right-hand ball in part (A), the rod will impart a negative charge to the ball. The right-hand ball will be charged negative with respect to the left-hand ball. When released, the two balls will be drawn together, as shown in figure 1-5 (A). They will touch and remain in contact until the left-hand ball acquires a portion of the negative charge of the right-hand ball, at which time they will swing apart as shown in figure 1-5 (C). If. positive charges are placed on both balls (fig. 1-5 (B)), the balls will also be repelled from each other.

COULOMB'S LAW OF CHARGES

The amount of attracting or repelling force which acts between two electrically charged bodies in free space depends on two things(1) their charges, and (2) the distance between them. The relationship of charge and distance to electrostatic force was first discovered and written by a French scientist named Charles A. Coulomb. Coulomb's Law states that CHARGED BODIES ATTRACT OR REPEL EACH OTHER WITH A FORCE THAT IS DIRECTLY PROPORTIONAL TO THE PRODUCT OF THEIR CHARGES, AND IS INVERSELY PROPORTIONAL TO THE SQUARE OF THE DISTANCE BETWEEN THEM.

ELECTRIC FIELDS

The space between and around charged bodies in which their influence is felt is called an ELECTRIC FIELD OF FORCE. The electric field is always terminated on material objects and extends between positive and negative charges. It can exist in air, glass, paper, or a vacuum. ELECTRO-STATIC FIELDS and DIELECTRIC FIELDS are other names used to refer to this region of force.

Fields of force spread out in the space surrounding their point of origin and, in general, DIMINISH IN PROPORTION TO THE SQUARE OF THE DISTANCE FROM THEIR SOURCE.

The field about a charged body is generally represented by lines which are

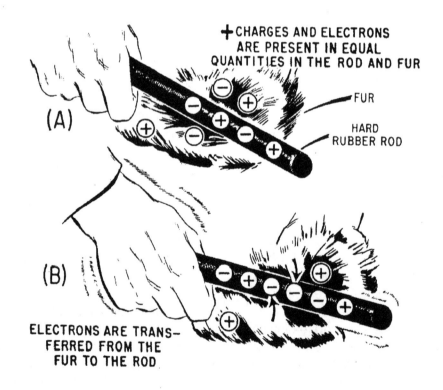

Figure 1-4.—Producing static electricity by friction.

referred to as ELECTROSTATIC LINES OF FORCE. These lines are imaginary and are used merely to represent the direction and strength of the field. To avoid confusion, the lines of force exerted by a positive charge are always shown leaving the charge, and for a negative charge they are shown as entering. Figure 1-6 illustrates the use of

lines to represent the field about charged bodies.

Figure 1-6 (A) represents the repulsion of like-charged bodies and their associated fields. Part (B) represents the attraction between unlike-charged bodies and their associated fields.

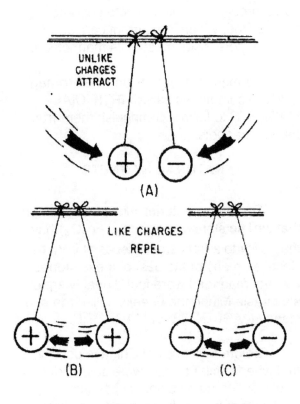

Figure 1-5.–Reaction between charged bodies.

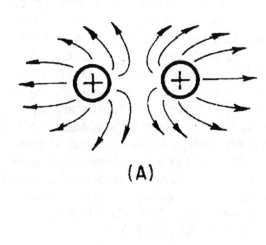

(A)

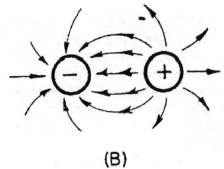

(B)

Figure 1-6.–Electrostatic lines of force.

Magnetism

A substance is said to be a magnet if it has the property of magnetism-that is, if it has the power to attract such substances as iron, steel, nickel, or cobalt, which are known as MAGNETIC MATERIALS. A steel knitting needle, magnetized by a method to be described later, exhibits two points of maximum attraction (one at each end) and no attraction at its center. The points of maximum attraction are called MAGNETIC POLES. All magnets have at least two poles. If the needle is suspended by its middle so that it rotates freely in a horizontal plane about its center, the needle comes to rest in an approximately north-south line of direction. The same pole will always point to the north, and the other will always point toward the south. The magnetic pole that points northward is called the NORTH POLE, and the other the SOUTH POLE.

A MAGNETIC FIELD exists around a simple bar magnet. The field consists of imaginary lines along which a MAGNETIC FORCE acts. These lines emanate from the north pole of the magnet, and enter the south pole, returning to the north pole through the magnet itself, thus forming closed loops.

A MAGNETIC CIRCUIT is a complete path through which magnetic lines of force may be established under the influence of a magnetizing force. Most magnetic circuits are composed largely of magnetic materials in order to contain the magnetic flux. These circuits are similar to the ELECTRIC CIRCUIT, which is a complete path through which current is caused to flow under the influence of an electromotive force.

Magnets may be conveniently divided into three groups.

1. NATURAL MAGNETS, found in the natural state in the form of a mineral called magnetite.

2. PERMANENT MAGNETS, bars of hardened steel (or some form of alloy such as alnico) that have been permanently magnetized.

3. ELECTROMAGNETS, composed of soft-iron cores around which are wound coils of insulated wire. When an electric current flows through the coil, the core becomes magnetized. When the current ceases to flow, the core loses most of its magnetism.

Permanent magnets and electromagnets are sometimes called ARTIFICIAL MAGNETS to further distinguish them from natural magnets.

NATURAL MAGNETS

For many centuries it has been known that certain stones (magnetite, Fe_3O_4) have the ability to attract small pieces of iron. Because many of the best of these stones (natural magnets) were found near Magnesia in Asia Minor, the Greeks called the substance MAGNETITE, or MAGNETIC.

Before this, ancient Chinese observed that when similar stones were suspended freely, or floated on a light substance in a container of water, they tended to assume a nearly north-and-south position. Probably Chinese navigators used bits of magnetite floating on wood in a liquid-filled vessel as crude compasses. At that time it was not known that the earth itself acts like a magnet, and these stones were regarded with considerable superstitious awe. Because bits of this substance were used as compasses they were called LOADSTONES (or lodestones), which means "leading stones."

Natural magnets are also found in the United States, Norway, and Sweden. A natural magnet, demonstrating the attractive force at the poles, is shown in figure 1-7 (A).

ARTIFICIAL MAGNETS

Natural magnets no longer have any practical value because more powerful and more conveniently shaped permanent magnets can be produced artificially. Commercial magnets are made from special steels and alloysfor example, alnico, made principally of aluminum, nickel, and cobalt. The name is derived from the first two letters of the three principal elements of which it is composed. An artificial magnet is shown in figure 1-7 (B).

An iron, steel, or alloy bar can be magnetized by inserting the bar into a coil of insulated wire and passing a heavy direct current through the coil, as shown in figure 1-8 (A). This aspect of magnetism is

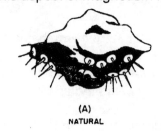

(A)
NATURAL

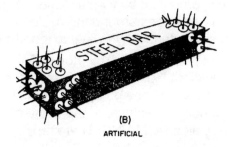

(B)
ARTIFICIAL

Figure 1-7.–(A) Natural magnet; (B) artificial magnet.

treated later in the chapter. The same bar may also be magnetized if it is stroked with a bar magnet, as shown in figure 1-8 (B). It will then have the same magnetic property that the magnet used to induce the magnetism-has namely, there will be two poles of attraction, one at either end. This process produces a permanent magnet by INDUCTION-that is, the magnetism is induced in the bar by the influence of the stroking magnet.

Artificial magnets may be classified as "permanent" or "temporary" depending on their ability to retain their magnetic strength after the magnetizing force has been removed. Hardened steel and certain alloys are relatively difficult to magnetize and are said to have a LOW PERMEABILITY because the magnetic lines of force do not easily permeate, or distribute themselves readily through the steel. Once magnetized, however, these materials retain a large part of their magnetic strength and are called PERMANENT MAGNETS. Permanent magnets are used extensively in electric instruments, meters, telephone receivers, permanent-magnet loudspeakers, andmagnetos. Conversely, substances

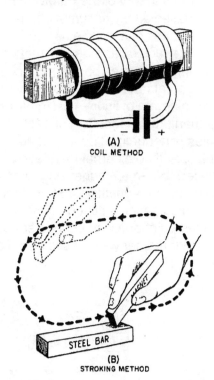

(A)
COIL METHOD

(B)
STROKING METHOD

Figure 1-8.Methods of producing artificial magnets.

that are relatively easy to magnetizesuch as soft iron and annealed silicon steelare said to have a HIGH PERMEABILITY. Such substances retain only a small part of their magnetism after the magnetizing force is removed and are called TEMPORARY MAGNETS. Silicon steel and similar materials are used in transformers where the magnetism is constantly changing and in generators and motors where the strengths of the fields can be readily changed.

The magnetism that remains in a temporary magnet after the magnetizing force is removed is called RESIDUAL MAGNETISM. The fact that temporary magnets retain even a small amount of magnetism is an important factor in the buildup of voltage in self-excited d-c generators.

NATURE OF MAGNETISM

Weber's theory of the nature of magnetism is based on the assumption that each of the molecules of a magnet is itself a tiny magnet. The molecular magnets that compose an unmagne-tized bar of iron or steel are arranged at random, as shown by the simplified diagram of figure 1-9 (A). With this arrangement, the magnetism of each of the molecules is neutralized by that of adjacent molecules, and no external magnetic effect is produced. When a magnetizing force is applied to an unmagnetized iron or steel bar, the molecules become alined so that the north poles point one way and the south poles point the other way, as shown in figure 1-9 (B).

same. If this breaking process could be continued, smaller and smaller pieces would retain their magnetism until each part was reduced to a molecule. It is therefore logical to assume that each of these molecules is a magnet.

A further justification for this assumption results from the fact that when a bar magnet is held out of alinement with the earth's field and is repeatedly jarred, heated, or exposed to a powerful alternating field, the molecular alinement is disarranged and the magnet becomes demagnetized. For example, electric measuring instruments become inaccurate if their permanent magnets lose some of their magnetism because of severe jarring or exposure to opposing magnetic fields.

A theory of magnetism that is perhaps more adequate than the MOLECULAR theory is the DOMAIN theory. Much simplified, this theory may be stated as follows:

In magnetic substances the "atomic" magnets, produced by the movement of the planetary electrons around the nucleus, have a strong tendency to line up together in groups of from 10^{14} to 10^{15} atoms. This occurs without the influence of any external magnetic field. These groups of atoms having their poles orientated in the same direction are called DOMAINS. Therefore,

 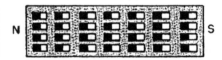

UNMAGNETIZED STEEL (A)   MAGNETIZED STEEL (B)

Figure 1-9.—Molecular theory of magnetism.

If a bar magnet is broken into several parts, as in figure 1-10, each part constitutes a magnet. The north and south poles of these small magnets are in the same respective directions as those of the original magnet. If each of these parts is again broken, the resulting parts are likewise magnets, and the magnetic orientation is the

throughout each domain an intense magnetic field is produced. These fields are normally in a miscellaneous arrangement so that no external field is apparent when the substance as a whole is unmagnetized. Each tiny domain (10^6 of them may be contained in 1 cubic millimeter) is always magnetized to saturation, and the addition of an external magnetic field does not increase the inherent magnetism of the individual domains.

However, if an external field that is gradually increased in strength is applied to the magnetic substance the domains will line up one by one (or perhaps several at a time) with the external field.

MAGNETIC FIELDS AND LINES OF FORCE

If a bar magnet is dipped into iron filings, many of the filings are attracted to the ends of the magnet, but none are attracted to the center of the magnet. As mentioned previously, the ends of the magnet where the attractive force is the greatest are called the POLES of the magnet. By using a compass, the line of direction of the magnetic force at various points near the magnet may be observed. The compass needle itself is a magnet. The north end of the compass needle always points toward the south pole, S, as shown in figure 1-11 (A), and thus the sense of direction (with respect to the polarity of the bar magnet) is also indicated. At the center, the compass needle points in a direction that is parallel to the bar magnet.

When the compass is placed successively at several points in the vicinity of the bar magnet the compass needle alines itself with the field at each position. The direction of the field is indicated by the arrows and represents the direction in which the north pole of the compass needle will point when the compass is placed in this field. Such a line along which a compass needle alines itself is called a MAGNETIC LINE OF FORCE. As mentioned previously, the magnetic lines of force are assumed to emanate from the north pole of a magnet, pass through the surrounding space, and enter

the south pole. The lines of force then pass from the south pole to the north pole inside the magnet to form a closed loop. Each line of force forms an independent closed loop and does not merge with or cross other lines of force. The lines of force between the poles of a horseshoe magnet are shown in figure 1-11 (B).

The space surrounding a magnet, in which the magnetic force acts, is called a MAGNETIC FIELD. Michael Faraday was the first scientist to visualize the magnet field as being in a state of stress and consisting of uniformly distributed lines of force. The entire quantity of magnetic lines surrounding a magnet is called MAGNETIC FLUX. Flux in a magnetic circuit corresponds to current in an electric circuit.

The number of lines of force per unit area is called FLUX DENSITY and is measured in lines per square inch or lines per square centimeter. Flux density is expressed by the equation

$$B = \frac{\phi}{A}$$

where B is the flux density, ϕ (Greek phi) is the total number of lines of flux, and A is the cross-sectional area of the magnetic circuit. If A is in square centimeters, B is in lines per square centimeter, or GAUSS. The terms FLUX and FLOW of magnetism are frequently used in textbooks. However, magnetism itself is not thought to be a stream of particles in motion, but is simply a field of force exerted in space. A visual representation pf the magnetic field around a magnet can be obtained by placing a plate of glass over a magnet and sprinkling iron filings onto

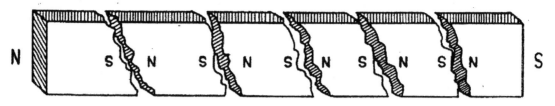

Figure 1-10.—Magnetic poles of a broken magnet.

the glass. The filings arrange themselves in definite paths between the poles.

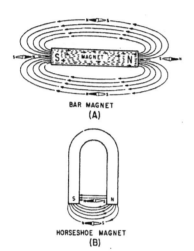

BAR MAGNET
(A)

HORSESHOE MAGNET
(B)

Figure 1-11.—Magnetic lines of force.

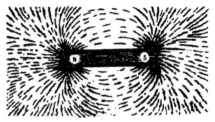

Figure 1-12.—Magnetic field pattern around a magnet.

Thus, the first two laws of magnetic attraction and repulsion are:

    1. LIKE magnetic poles REPEL each other.

    2. UNLIKE magnetic poles ATTRACT each other.

This arrangement of the filings shows the pattern of the magnetic field around the magnet, as in figure 1-12.

The magnetic field surrounding a symmetrically shaped magnet has the following properties:

    1. The field is symmetrical unless disturbed by another magnetic substance.

    2. The lines of force have direction and are represented as emanating from the north pole and entering the south pole.

LAWS OF ATTRACTION AND REPULSION

If a magnetized needle is suspended near a bar magnet, as in figure 1-13, it will be seen that a north pole repels a north pole and a south pole repels a south pole. Opposite poles, however, will attract each other.

The flux patterns between adjacent UNLIKE poles of bar magnets, as indicated by lines, are shown in figure 1-14 (A). Similar patterns for adjacent LIKE poles are shown in figure 1-14 (B). The lines do not cross at any point and they act as if they repel each other.

Figure 1-15 shows the flux pattern (indicated by lines) around two bar magnets placed close together and parallel with each other. Figure 1-15 (A) shows the flux pattern when opposite poles are adjacent; and figure 1-15 (B) shows the flux pattern when like poles are adjacent.

The THIRD LAW of magnetic attraction and repulsion states in effect that the force of attraction or repulsion existing between two magnetic poles decreases rapidly as the poles are separated from each other. Actually, the force of attraction or repulsion varies directly as the product of the separate pole strengths and inversely as the square of the distance separating the magnetic

poles, provided the poles are small enough to be considered as points. For example, if the distance between two north poles is increased from 2 feet to 4 feet, the force of

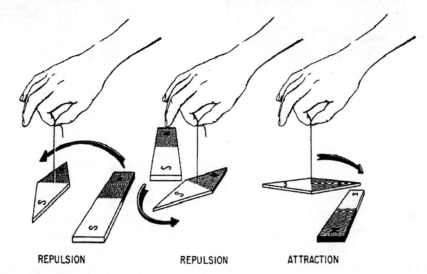

REPULSION   REPULSION   ATTRACTION

Figure 1-13.—Laws of attraction and repulsion.

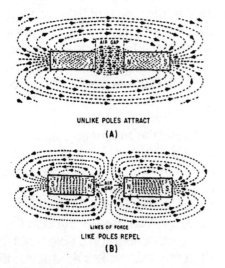

UNLIKE POLES ATTRACT
(A)

LINES OF FORCE
LIKE POLES REPEL
(B)

Figure 1-14.—Lines of force between unlike and like poles.

end of the axis of rotation of the earth. The magnetic axis does not coincide with the geographic axis, and therefore the magnetic and geographic poles are not at the same place on the surface of the earth.

The early users of the compass regarded the end of the compass needle that points in a northerly direction as being a north pole. The other end was regarded as a south pole. On some maps the magnetic pole of the earth towards which the north pole of the compass pointed was designated a north magnetic pole. This magnetic pole was obviously called a north pole because of its proximity to the north geographic pole.

repulsion between them is decreased to one-fourth of its original value. If either pole strength is doubled, the distance remaining the same, the force between the poles will be doubled.

THE EARTH'S MAGNETISM

As has been stated, the earth is a huge magnet; and surrounding the earth is the magnetic field produced by the earth's magnetism. The magnetic polarities of the earth are as indicated in figure 1-16. The geographic poles are also shown at each

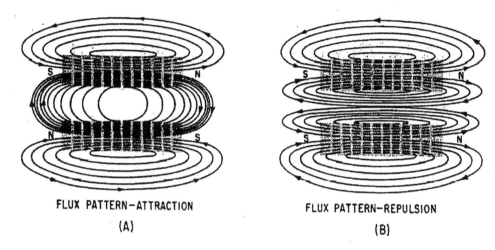

FLUX PATTERN—ATTRACTION

(A)

FLUX PATTERN—REPULSION

(B)

Figure 1-15.—Flux patterns of adjacent parallel bar magnets.

When it was learned that the earth is a magnet and that opposite poles attract, it was necessary to call the magnetic pole located in the northern hemisphere a SOUTH MAGNETIC POLE and the magnetic pole located in the southern hemisphere a NORTH MAGNETIC POLE. The matter of naming the poles was arbitrary. Obviously, the polarity of the compass needle that points toward the north must be opposite to the polarity of the earth's magnetic pole located there.

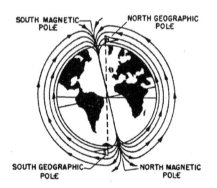

Figure 1-16.—Earth's magnetic poles.

As has been stated, magnetic lines of force are assumed to emanate from the north pole of a magnet and to enter the south pole as closed loops. Because the earth is a magnet, lines of force emanate

from its north magnetic pole and enter the south magnetic pole as closed loops. The compass needle alines itself in such a way that the earth's lines of force enter at its south pole and leave at its north pole. Because the north pole of the needle is defined as the end that points in a northerly direction it follows that the magnetic pole in the vicinity of the north geographic pole is in reality a south magnetic pole, and vice versa.

Because the magnetic poles and the geographic poles do not coincide, a compass will not (except at certain positions on the earth) point in a true (geographic) north-south direction-that is, it will not point in a line of direction that passes through the north and south geographic poles, but in a line of direction that makes an angle with it. This angle is called the angle of VARIATION OR DECLINATION.

MAGNETIC SHIELDING

There is not a known INSULATOR for magnetic flux. If a nonmagnetic material is placed in a magnetic field, there is no appreciable change in flux-that is, the flux penetrates the nonmagnetic material. For example, a glass plate placed between the poles of a horseshoe magnet will have no appreciable effect on the field although glass itself is a good insulator in an electric circuit. If a magnetic material (for example, soft iron) is placed in a magnetic field, the flux may be redirected to take advantage of the greater permeability of the magnetic material as shown in figure 1-17. Permeability is the quality of a substance which determines the ease with which it can be magnetized.

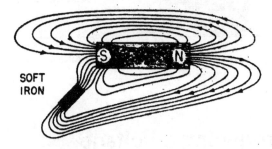

Figure 1-17.—Effects of a magnetic substance in a magnetic field.

The sensitive mechanism of electric instruments and meters can be influenced by stray magnetic fields which will cause errors in their readings. Because instrument mechanisms cannot be insulated against magnetic flux, it is necessary to employ some means of directing the flux around the instrument. This is accomplished by placing a soft-iron case, called a MAGNETIC SCREEN OR SHIELD, about the instrument. Because the flux *is* established more readily through the iron (even though the path is longer) than through the air inside the case, the instrument is effectively shielded, as shown by the watch and soft-iron shield in figure 1-18.

The study of electricity and magnetism, and how they affect each other, is given more thorough coverage in later chapters of this course.

The discussion of magnetism up to this point has been mainly intended to clarify terms and meanings, such as "polarity," "fields," "lines of force," and so forth. Only one fundamental relationship between magnetism and electricity is discussed in this chapter. This relationship pertains to magnetism as used to generate a voltage and it is discussed under the headings that follows.

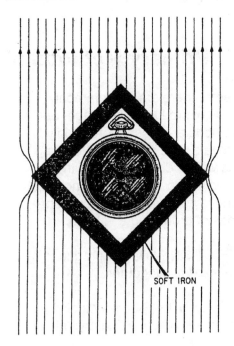

SOFT IRON

Figure 1-18.—Magnetic shield.

Difference in Potential

The force that causes free electrons to move in a conductor as an electric current is called (1) an electromotive force (e.m.f.), (2) a voltage, or (3) a difference in potential. When a difference in potential exists between two charged bodies that are connected by a conductor, electrons will flow along the conductor. This flow will be from the negatively charged body to the positively charged body until the two charges are equalized and the potential difference no longer exists.

An analogy of this action is shown in the two water tanks connected by a pipe and valve in figure 1-19. At first the valve is closed and all the water is in tank A. Thus, the water pressure across the valve is at maximum. When the valve is opened, the water flows through the pipe from A to B until the water level becomes the same in both tanks. The water then stops flowing in the pipe, because there is no longer a difference in water pressure between the two tanks.

Current flow through an electric circuit is directly proportional to the difference in potential across the circuit, just as the flow of water through the pipe in figure 1-19 is directly proportional to the difference in water level in the two tanks.

A fundamental law of current electricity is that the CURRENT IS DIRECTLY PROPORTIONAL TO THE APPLIED VOLT-AGE.

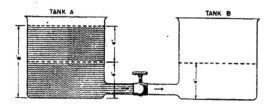

Figure 1-19.—Water analogy of electric difference in potential.

Primary Methods of Producing a Voltage

Presently, there are six commonly used methods of producing a voltage. Some of these methods are much more widely used than others. The methods of utilizing each source will be discussed, and their most common applications will be included. The following is a list of the six most common methods of producing a voltage.

1. FRICTION.-Voltage produced by rubbing two materials together.

2. PRESSURE (Piezoelectricity).-Voltage produced by squeezing crystals of certain substances.

3. HEAT (Thermoelectricity).-Voltage produced by heating the joint (junction) where two unlike metals are joined.

4. LIGHT (Photoelectricity).-Voltage produced by light striking photosensitive (light sensitive) substances.

5. CHEMICAL ACTION.-Voltage produced by chemical reaction in a battery cell.

6. MAGNETISM.-Voltage produced in a conductor when the conductor moves through a magnetic field, or a magnetic field moves through the conductor in such a manner as to cut the magnetic lines of force of the field.

VOLTAGE PRODUCED BY FRICTION

This is the least used of the six methods of producing voltages. Its main application is in Van de Graf generators, used by some laboratories to produce high voltages. As a rule, friction electricity (often referred to as static electricity) is a nuisance. For instance, a flying aircraft accumulates electric charges from the friction between its skin and the passing air.

These charges often interfere with radio communication, and under some circumstances can even cause physical damage to the aircraft. You have probably received unpleasant shocks from friction electricity upon sliding across dry seat covers or walking across dry carpets, and then coming in contact with some other object.

VOLTAGE PRODUCED BY PRESSURE

This action is referred to as piezoelectricity. It is produced by compressing or decompressing crystals of certain substances. To study this form of electricity, you must first understand the meaning of the word "crystal." In a crystal, the molecules are arranged in an orderly and uniform manner. A substance in its crystallized state and in its noncrystallized state is shown in figure 1-20.

For the sake of simplicity, assume that the molecules of this particular substance are spherical (ball-shaped). In the noncrystallized state, in part (A), note that the molecules are arranged irregularly. In the crystallized state, part (B), the molecules are arranged in a regular and uniform manner. This illustrates the major physical difference between crystal and noncrystal forms of matter. Natural crystalline matter is rare; an example of matter that is crystalline in its natural form is diamond, which is crystalline carbon. Most crystals are manufactured.

Crystals of certain substances, such as Rochelle salt or quartz, exhibit peculiar electrical characteristics. These characteristics, or effects, are referred to as "piezoelectric." For instance, when a crystal of quartz is compressed, as in figure 1-20 (C), electrons tend

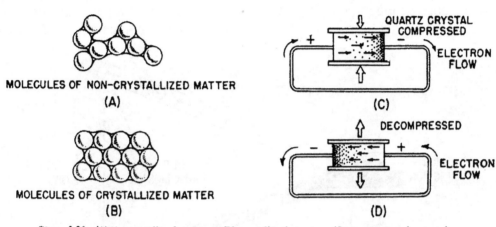

MOLECULES OF NON-CRYSTALLIZED MATTER
(A)

MOLECULES OF CRYSTALLIZED MATTER
(B)

Figure 1-20.—(A) Noncrystallized structure, (B) crystallized structure, (C) compression of a crystal, (D) decompression of a crystal.

to move through the crystal as shown. This tendency creates an electric difference of potential between the two opposite faces of the crystal. (The fundamental reasons for this action are not known. However, the action is predictable, and therefore useful.) If an external wire is connected while the pressure and e.m.f. are present, electrons will flow. If the pressure is held constant, the electron flow will continue until the charges are equalized. When the force is removed, the crystal is decompressed, and immediately causes an electric force in the opposite direction, as shown in part (D). Thus, the crystal is able to convert mechanical force, either pressure or tension, to electrical force.

The power capacity of a crystal is extremely small. However, they are useful because of their extreme sensitivity to changes of mechanical force or changes in temperature. Due to other characteristics not mentioned here, crystals are most widely used in radio communication equipment. The more complicated study of crystals, as they are used for practical applications, is left for those courses that pertain to the special ratings concerned with them.

VOLTAGE PRODUCED BY HEAT

When a length of metal, such as copper, is heated at one end, electrons tend to move away from the hot end toward the cooler end. This is true of most metals. However, in some metals, such as iron, the opposite takes place and electrons tend to move TOWARD the hot end. These characteristics are illustrated in figure 1-21. The negative charges (electrons) are moving through the copper away from the heat and through the iron toward the heat. They cross from the iron to the copper at the hot junction, and from the copper through the current meter to the iron at the cold junction. This device is generally referred to as a thermocouple.

18

Thermocouples have somewhat greater power capacities than crystals, but their capacity is still very small if compared to some other sources. The thermoelectric voltage in a thermocouple depends mainly on the difference in temperature between the hot and cold junctions. Consequently, they are widely used to measure temperature, and as heat-sensing devices in automatic temperature control equipment. Thermocouples generally can be subjected to much greater temperatures than ordinary thermometers, such as the mercury or alcohol types.

VOLTAGE PRODUCED BY LIGHT

When light strikes the surface of a substance, it may dislodge electrons from their orbits around the surface atoms of the substance. This occurs because light has energy, the same as any moving force.

Some substances, mostly metallic ones, are far more sensitive to light than others. That is, more electrons will be dislodged and emitted from the surface of a highly sensitive metal, with a given amount of light, than will be emitted from a less sensitive

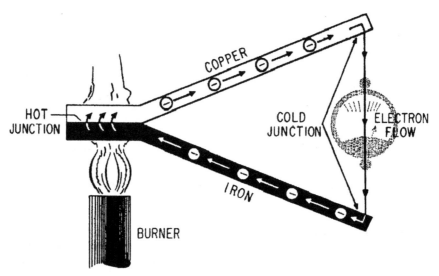

Figure 1-21.—Voltage produced by heat.

substance. Upon losing electrons, the photosensitive (light sensitive) metal becomes positively charged, and an electric force is created. Voltage produced in this manner is referred to as "a photoelectric voltage."

The photosensitive materials most commonly used to produce a photoelectric voltage are various compounds of silver oxide or copper oxide. A complete device which operates on the photoelectric principle is referred to as a "photoelectric cell." There are many sizes and types of photoelectric cells in use, each of which serves the special purpose for which it was designed. Nearly all, however, have some of the basic

features of the photoelectric cells shown in figure 1-22.

The cell shown in part (A) has a curved light-sensitive surface focused on the central anode. When light from the direction shown strikes the sensitive surface, it emits electrons toward the anode. The more intense the light, the greater is the number of electrons emitted. When a wire is connected between the filament and the back, or dark side, the accumulated electrons will flow to the dark side. These electrons will eventually

19

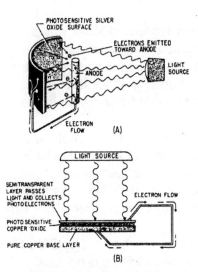

Figure 1-22.—Voltage produced by light.

the copper oxide. This additional layer serves two purposes:

1. It is EXTREMELY thin to permit the penetration of light to the copper oxide.

2. It also accumulates the electrons emitted by the copper oxide.

An externally connected wire completes the electron path, the same as in the reflector type cell. The photocell's voltage is utilized as needed by connecting the external wires to some other device, which amplifies (enlarges) it to a usable level.

A photocell's power capacity is very small. However, it reacts to light-intensity variations in an extremely short time. This characteristic makes the photocell very useful in detecting or accurately controlling a great number of processes or operations. For instance, the photoelectric cell, or some form of the photoelectric principle, is used in television cameras, automatic manufacturing process controls, door openers, burglar alarms, and so forth.

pass through the metal of the reflector and replace the electrons leaving the light-sensitive surface. Thus, light energy is converted to a flow of electrons, and a usable current is developed.

The cell shown in part (B) is constructed in layers. A base plate of pure copper is coated with light-sensitive copper oxide. An additional layer of metal is put over

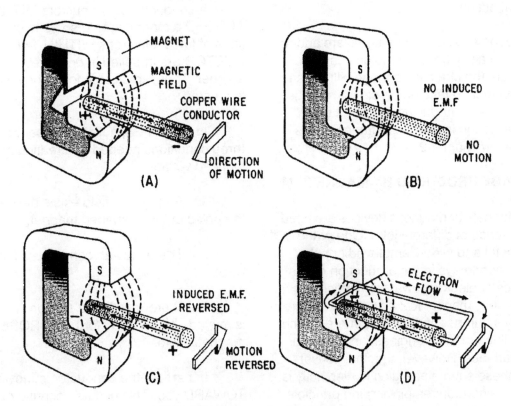

Figure 1-23.—Voltage produced by magnetism.

VOLTAGE PRODUCED BY CHEMICAL ACTION

Up to this point, it has been shown that electrons may be removed from their parent atoms and set in motion by energy derived from a source of friction, pressure, heat, or light. In general, these forms of energy do not alter the molecules of the substances being acted upon. That is, molecules are not usually added, taken away, or split-up when subjected to these four forms of energy. Only electrons are involved. When the molecules of a substance are altered, the action is referred to as CHEMICAL. For instance, if the molecules of a substance combines with atoms of another substance, or gives up atoms of its own, the action is chemical in nature. Such action always changes the , chemical name and characteristics of the substance affected. For instance, when atoms of oxygen from the air come in contact with bare iron, they merge with the molecules of iron. This iron is "oxidized." It has changed chemically from iron to iron oxide, or "rust." Its molecules have been altered by chemical action.

In some cases, when atoms are added to or taken away from the molecules of a substance, the chemical change will cause the substance to take on an electric charge. The process of producing a voltage by chemical action is used in batteries and is explained in chapter 2.

VOLTAGE PRODUCED BY MAGNETISM

Magnets or magnetic devices are used for thousands of different jobs. One of the most useful and widely employed applications of magnets is in the production of vast quantities of electric power from mechanical sources. The mechanical power may be provided by a number of different sources, such as gasoline or diesel engines, and water or steam turbines. However, the final conversion of these source energies to electricity is done by generators employing the principle of electromagnetic induction. These genera-

tors, of many types and sizes, are discussed in later chapters of this course. The important subject to be discussed here is the fundamental operating principle of ALL such electromagnetic-induction generators.

To begin with, there are three fundamental conditions which must exist before a voltage can be produced by magnetism. You should learn them well, because they will be encountered again and again. They are:

1. There must be a CONDUCTOR, in which the voltage will be produced.

2. There must be a MAGNETIC FIELD in the conductor's vicinity.

3. There must be relative motion between the field and the conductor. The conductor must be moved so as to cut across the magnetic lines of force, or the field must be moved so that the lines of force are cut by the conductor.

In accordance with these conditions, when a conductor or conductors MOVE ACROSS a magnetic field so as to cut the lines of force, electrons WITHIN THE CONDUCTOR are impelled in one direction or another. Thus, an electric force, or voltage, is created.

In figure 1-23, note the presence of the three conditions needed for creating an induced voltage:

1. A magnetic field exists between the poles of the C-shaped magnet.

2. There is a conductor (copper wire).

3. There is relative motion. The wire is moved back and forth ACROSS the magnetic field.

In part (A) the conductor is moving TOWARD you. This occurs because of the magnetically induced electromotive force (e.m.f.) acting on the electrons in the copper. The right-hand end becomes negative, and the left-hand end positive. In part (B) the conductor is stopped. This eliminates motion, one of the three required conditions, and there is no longer an induced e.m.f. Consequently, there is no longer any difference in potential between the two ends of the wire. In part (C) the conductor is moving AWAY from you. An induced e.m.f. is again created. However, note carefully that the REVERSAL OF MOTION has caused a REVERSAL OF DIRECTION in the induced e.m.f.

If a path for electron flow is provided between the ends of the conductor, elec-

trons will leave the negative end and flow to the positive end. This condition is shown in part (D). Electron flow will continue as long as the e.m.f. exists. In studying figure 1-23, it should be noted that the induced e.m.f. could also have been created by holding the conductor stationary and moving the magnetic field back and forth.

In later chapters of this course, under the heading "Generators," you will study the more complex aspects of power generation by use of mechanical motion and magnetism.

Electric Current

The drift or flow of electrons through a conductor is called ELECTRIC CURRENT. In order to determine the amount (number) of electrons flowing in a given conductor, it is necessary to adopt a unit of measurement of current flow. The term AMPERE is used to define the unit of measurement of the rate at which current flows (electron flow). The symbol for the ampere is I. One ampere may be defined as the flow of 6.28×10^{18} electrons per second past a fixed point in a conductor

A unit quantity of electricity is moved through an electric circuit when one ampere of current flows for one second of time. This unit is equivalent to 6.28×10^{18} electrons, and is called the COULOMB. The coulomb is to electricity as the gallon is to water. The symbol for the coulomb is Q. The rate of flow of current in amperes and the quantity of electricity moved through a circuit are related by the common factor of time. Thus,

the quantity of electric charge, in coulombs, electricity moved through a circuit are is equal to the product of the current in amperes, I, and the duration of flow in seconds, t. Expressed as an equation, $Q = It$.

For example, if a current of 2 amperes flows through a circuit for 10 seconds the quantity of electricity moved through the circuit is 2 x 10, or 20 coulombs. Conversely, current flow may be expressed in terms of coulombs and time in seconds. Thus, if 20 coulombs are moved through a circuit in 10 seconds, the average current flow is 20/10, or 2 amperes. Note that the current flow in amperes implies the rate of flow of coulombs per second without indicating either coulombs or seconds. Thus a current flow of 2 amperes is equivalent to a rate of flow of 2 coulombs per second.

Resistance

Every material offers some resistance, or opposition, to the flow of electric cur rent through it. Good conductors, such as copper, silver, and aluminum, offer very little resistance. Poor conductors, or insulators, such as glass, wood, and paper, offer a high resistance to current flow.

The size and type of material of the wires in an electric circuit are chosen so as to keep the electrical resistance as low as possible. In this way, current can flow easily through the conductors, just as water flows through the pipe between the tanks in figure 1-19. If the water pressure remains constant the flow of water in the pipe will depend on how far the valve is opened. The smaller the opening, the greater the opposition to the flow, and the smaller will be the rate of flow in gallons per second.

In the electric circuit, the larger the diameter of the wires, the lower will be their electrical resistance (opposition) to the flow of current through them. In the water analogy, pipe friction opposes the flow of water between the tanks. This friction is similar to electrical resistance. The resistance of the pipe to the flow of water through it depends upon (1) the length of the pipe, (2) the diameter of the pipe, and (3) the nature of the inside walls (rough or smooth). Similarly, the electrical resistance of the conductors depends upon (1) the length of the wires, (2) the diameter of the wires, and (3) the material of the wires (copper, aluminum, etc.).

Temperature also affects the resistance of electrical conductors to some extent. In most conductors (copper, aluminum, iron, etc.) the resistance increases with temperature. Carbon is an exception. In carbon the resistance decreases as temperature increases. Certain alloys of metals (manganin and constantan) have resistance that does not change appreciably with temperature.

The relative resistance of several conductors of the same length and cross section is given in the following list with silver as a standard of 1 and the remaining metals arranged in an order of ascending resistance:

Silver...............	1.0
Copper.............	1.08
Gold...............	1.4
Aluminum...........	1.8
Platinum............	7.0
Lead..............	13.5

The resistance in an electrical circuit is expressed by the symbol R. Manufactured circuit parts containing definite amounts of resistance are called RESISTORS. Resistance (R) is measured in OHMS. One ohm is the resistance of a circuit element, or circuit, that permits a steady current of 1 ampere (1 coulomb per second) to flow when a steady e.m.f. of 1 volt is applied to the circuit.

ELECTRICAL TERMS AND FORMULAS

CONTENTS

ELECTRICAL TERMS AND FORMULAS

Terms

AGONIC.—An imaginary line of the earth's surface passing through points where the magnetic declination is 0°; that is, points where the compass points to true north.

AMMETER.—An instrument for measuring the amount of electron flow in amperes.

AMPERE.—The basic unit of electrical current.

AMPERE-TURN.—The magnetizing force produced by a current of one ampere flowing through a coil of one turn.

AMPLIDYNE.—A rotary magnetic or dynamo-electric amplifier used in servomechanism and control applications.

AMPLIFICATION.—The process of increasing the strength (current, power, or voltage) of a signal.

AMPLIFIER.—A device used to increase the signal voltage, current, or power, generally composed of a vacuum tube and associated circuit called a stage. It may contain several stages in order to obtain a desired gain.

AMPLITUDE.—The maximum instantaneous value of an alternating voltage or current, measured in either the positive or negative direction.

ARC.—A flash caused by an electric current ionizing a gas or vapor.

ARMATURE.—The rotating part of an electric motor or generator. The moving part of a relay or vibrator.

ATTENUATOR.—A network of resistors used to reduce voltage, current, or power delivered to a load.

AUTOTRANSFORMER.—A transformer in which the primary and secondary are connected together in one winding.

BATTERY.—Two or more primary or secondary cells connected together electrically. The term does not apply to a single cell.

BREAKER POINTS.—Metal contacts that open and close a circuit at timed intervals.

BRIDGE CIRCUIT.—The electrical bridge circuit is a term referring to any one of a variety of electric circuit networks, one branch of which, the "bridge" proper, connects two points of equal potential and hence carries no current when the circuit is properly adjusted or balanced.

BRUSH.—The conducting material, usually a block of carbon, bearing against the commutator or sliprings through which the current flows in or out.

BUS BAR.—A primary power distribution point connected to the main power source.

CAPACITOR.—Two electrodes or sets of electrodes in the form of plates, separated from each other by an insulating material called the dielectric.

CHOKE COIL.—A coil of low ohmic resistance and high impedance to alternating current.

CIRCUIT.—The complete path of an electric current.

CIRCUIT BREAKER.—An electromagnetic or thermal device that opens a circuit when the current in the circuit exceeds a predetermined amount. Circuit breakers can be reset.

CIRCULAR MIL.—An area equal to that of a circle with a diameter of 0.001 inch. It is used for measuring the cross section of wires.

COAXIAL CABLE.—A transmission line consisting of two conductors concentric with and insulated from each other.

COMMUTATOR.—The copper segments on the armature of a motor or generator. It is cylindrical in shape and is used to pass power into or from the brushes. It is a switching device.

CONDUCTANCE.—The ability of a material to conduct or carry an electric current. It is the reciprocal of the resistance of the material, and is expressed in mhos.

CONDUCTIVITY.—The ease with which a substance transmits electricity.

CONDUCTOR.—Any material suitable for carrying electric current.

CORE.—A magnetic material that affords an easy path for magnetic flux lines in a coil.

COUNTER E.M.F.—Counter electromotive force; an e.m.f. induced in a coil or armature that opposes the applied voltage.

CURRENT LIMITER.—A protective device similar to a fuse, usually used in high amperage circuits.

CYCLE.—One complete positive and one complete negative alternation of a current or voltage.

DIELECTRIC.—An insulator; a term that refers to the insulating material between the plates of a capacitor.

DIODE.—Vacuum tube—a two element tube that contains a cathode and plate; semiconductor—a material of either germanium or silicon that is manufactured to allow current to flow in only one direction. Diodes are used as rectifiers and detectors.

DIRECT CURRENT.—An electric current that flows in one direction only.

EDDY CURRENT.—Induced circulating currents in a conducting material that are caused by a varying magnetic field.

EFFICIENCY.—The ratio of output power to input power, generally expressed as a percentage.

ELECTROLYTE.—A solution of a substance which is capable of conducting electricity. An electrolyte may be in the form of either a liquid or a paste.

ELECTROMAGNET.—A magnet made by passing current through a coil of wire wound on a soft iron core.

ELECTROMOTIVE FORCE (e.m.f.).—The force that produces an electric current in a circuit.

ELECTRON.—A negatively charged particle of matter.

ENERGY.—The ability or capacity to do work.

FARAD.—The unit of capacitance.

FEEDBACK.—A transfer of energy from the output circuit of a device back to its input.

FIELD.—The space containing electric or magnetic lines of force.

FIELD WINDING.—The coil used to provide the magnetizing force in motors and generators.

FLUX FIELD.—All electric or magnetic lines of force in a given region.

FREE ELECTRONS.—Electrons which are loosely held and consequently tend to move at random among the atoms of the material.

FREQUENCY.—The number of complete cycles per second existing in any form of wave motion; such as the number of cycles per second of an alternating current.

FULL-WAVE RECTIFIER CIRCUIT.—A circuit which utilizes both the positive and the negative alternations of an alternating current to produce a direct current.

FUSE.—A protective device inserted in series with a circuit. It contains a metal that will melt or break when current is increased beyond a specific value for a definite period of time.

GAIN.—The ratio of the output power, voltage, or current to the input power, voltage, or current, respectively.

GALVANOMETER.—An instrument used to measure small d-c currents.

GENERATOR.—A machine that converts mechanical energy into electrical energy.

GROUND.—A metallic connection with the earth to establish ground potential. Also, a common return to a point of zero potential. The chassis of a receiver or a transmitter is sometimes the common return, and therefore the ground of the unit.

HENRY.—The basic unit of inductance.

HORSEPOWER.—The English unit of power, equal to work done at the rate of 550 foot-pounds per second. Equal to 746 watts of electrical power.

HYSTERESIS.—A lagging of the magnetic flux in a magnetic material behind the magnetizing force which is producing it.

IMPEDANCE.—The total opposition offered to the flow of an alternating current. It may consist of any combination of resistance, inductive reactance, and capacitive reactance.

INDUCTANCE.—The property of a circuit which tends to oppose a change in the existing current.

INDUCTION.—The act or process of producing voltage by the relative motion of a magnetic field across a conductor.

INDUCTIVE REACTANCE.—The opposition to the flow of alternating or pulsating current caused by the inductance of a circuit. It is measured in ohms.

INPHASE.—Applied to the condition that exists when two waves of the same frequency pass through their maximum and minimum values of like polarity at the same instant.

INVERSELY.—Inverted or reversed in position or relationship.

ISOGONIC LINE.—An imaginary line drawn through points on the earth's surface where the magnetic deviation is equal.

JOULE.—A unit of energy or work. A joule of energy is liberated by one ampere flowing for one second through a resistance of one ohm.

KILO.—A prefix meaning 1,000.

LAG.—The amount one wave is behind another in time; expressed in electrical degrees.

LAMINATED CORE.—A core built up from thin sheets of metal and used in transformers and relays.

LEAD.—The opposite of LAG. Also, a wire or connection.

LINE OF FORCE.–A line in an electric or magnetic field that shows the direction of the force.

LOAD.–The power that is being delivered by any power producing device. The equipment that uses the power from the power producing device.

MAGNETIC AMPLIFIER.–A saturable reactor type device that is used in a circuit to amplify or control.

MAGNETIC CIRCUIT.–The complete path of magnetic lines of force.

MAGNETIC FIELD.–The space in which a magnetic force exists.

MAGNETIC FLUX.–The total number of lines of force issuing from a pole of a magnet.

MAGNETIZE.–To convert a material into a magnet by causing the molecules to rearrange.

MAGNETO.–A generator which produces alternating current and has a permanent magnet as its field.

MEGGER.–A test instrument used to measure insulation resistance and other high resistances. It is a portable hand operated d-c generator used as an ohmmeter.

MEGOHM.–A million ohms.

MICRO.–A prefix meaning one-millionth.

MILLI.–A prefix meaning one-thousandth.

MILLIAMMETER.–An ammeter that measures current in thousandths of an ampere.

MOTOR-GENERATOR.–A motor and a generator with a common shaft used to convert line voltages to other voltages or frequencies.

MUTUAL INDUCTANCE.–A circuit property existing when the relative position of two inductors causes the magnetic lines of force from one to link with the turns of the other.

NEGATIVE CHARGE.–The electrical charge carried by a body which has an excess of electrons.

NEUTRON.–A particle having the weight of a proton but carrying no electric charge. It is located in the nucleus of an atom.

NUCLEUS.–The central part of an atom that is mainly comprised of protons and neutrons. It is the part of the atom that has the most mass.

NULL.–Zero.

OHM.–The unit of electrical resistance.

OHMMETER.–An instrument for directly measuring resistance in ohms.

OVERLOAD.–A load greater than the rated load of an electrical device.

PERMALLOY.–An alloy of nickel and iron having an abnormally high magnetic permeability.

PERMEABILITY.–A measure of the ease with which magnetic lines of force can flow through a material as compared to air.

PHASE DIFFERENCE.–The time in electrical degrees by which one wave leads or lags another.

POLARITY.–The character of having magnetic poles, or electric charges.

POLE.–The section of a magnet where the flux lines are concentrated; also where they enter and leave the magnet. An electrode of a battery.

POLYPHASE.–A circuit that utilizes more than one phase of alternating current.

POSITIVE CHARGE.–The electrical charge carried by a body which has become deficient in electrons.

POTENTIAL.–The amount of charge held by a body as compared to another point or body. Usually measured in volts.

POTENTIOMETER.–A variable voltage divider; a resistor which has a variable contact arm so that any portion of the potential applied between its ends may be selected.

POWER.–The rate of doing work or the rate of expending energy. The unit of electrical power is the watt.

POWER FACTOR.–The ratio of the actual power of an alternating or pulsating current, as measured by a wattmeter, to the apparent power, as indicated by ammeter and voltmeter readings. The power factor of an inductor, capacitor, or insulator is an expression of their losses.

PRIME MOVER.–The source of mechanical power used to drive the rotor of a generator.

PROTON.–A positively charged particle in the nucleus of an atom.

RATIO.–The value obtained by dividing one number by another, indicating their relative proportions.

REACTANCE.–The opposition offered to the flow of an alternating current by the inductance, capacitance, or both, in any circuit.

RECTIFIERS.–Devices used to change alternating current to unidirectional current. These may be vacuum tubes, semiconductors such as germanium and silicon, and dry-disk rectifiers such as selenium and copper-oxide.

RELAY.–An electromechanical switching device that can be used as a remote control.

RELUCTANCE.–A measure of the opposition that a material offers to magnetic lines of force.

RESISTANCE.–The opposition to the flow of current caused by the nature and physical dimensions of a conductor.

RESISTOR.–A circuit element whose chief characteristic is resistance; used to oppose the flow of current.

ELECTRICAL TERMS AND FORMULAS

RETENTIVITY.—The measure of the ability of a material to hold its magnetism.

RHEOSTAT.—A variable resistor.

SATURABLE REACTOR.—A control device that uses a small d-c current to control a large a-c current by controlling core flux density.

SATURATION.—The condition existing in any circuit when an increase in the driving signal produces no further change in the resultant effect.

SELF-INDUCTION.—The process by which a circuit induces an e.m.f. into itself by its own magnetic field.

SERIES-WOUND.—A motor or generator in which the armature is wired in series with the field winding.

SERVO.—A device used to convert a small movement into one of greater movement or force.

SERVOMECHANISM.—A closed-loop system that produces a force to position an object in accordance with the information that originates at the input.

SOLENOID.—An electromagnetic coil that contains a movable plunger.

SPACE CHARGE.—The cloud of electrons existing in the space between the cathode and plate in a vacuum tube, formed by the electrons emitted from the cathode in excess of those immediately attracted to the plate.

SPECIFIC GRAVITY—The ratio between the density of a substance and that of pure water, at a given temperature.

SYNCHROSCOPE—An instrument used to indicate a difference in frequency between two a-c sources.

SYNCHRO SYSTEM.—An electrical system that gives remote indications or control by means of self-synchronizing motors.

TACHOMETER.—An instrument for indicating revolutions per minute.

TERTIARY WINDING.—A third winding on a transformer or magnetic amplifier that is used as a second control winding.

THERMISTOR.—A resistor that is used to compensate for temperature variations in a circuit.

THERMOCOUPLE.—A junction of two dissimilar metals that produces a voltage when heated.

TORQUE.—The turning effort or twist which a shaft sustains when transmitting power.

TRANSFORMER.—A device composed of two or more coils, linked by magnetic lines of force, used to transfer energy from one circuit to another.

TRANSMISSION LINES.—Any conductor or system of conductors used to carry electrical energy from its source to a load.

VARS.—Abbreviation for volt-ampere, reactive.

VECTOR.—A line used to represent both direction and magnitude.

VOLT.—The unit of electrical potential.

VOLTMETER.—An instrument designed to measure a difference in electrical potential, in volts.

WATT.—The unit of electrical power.

WATTMETER.—An instrument for measuring electrical power in watts.

Formulas

Ohm's Law for d-c Circuits

$$I = \frac{E}{R} = \frac{P}{E} = \sqrt{\frac{P}{R}}$$

$$R = \frac{E}{I} = \frac{P}{I^2} = \frac{E^2}{P}$$

$$E = IR = \frac{P}{I} = \sqrt{PR}$$

$$P = EI = \frac{E^2}{R} = I^2R$$

Resistors in Series

$$R_T = R_1 + R_2 \dots$$

Resistors in Parallel
Two resistors

$$R_T = \frac{R_1 R_2}{R_1 + R_2}$$

More than two

$$\frac{1}{R_T} = \frac{1}{R_1} + \frac{1}{R_2} + \frac{1}{R_3}$$

ELECTRICAL TERMS AND FORMULAS

R-L Circuit Time Constant equals

$$\frac{L \text{ (in henrys)}}{R \text{ (in ohms)}} = t \text{ (in seconds), or}$$

$$\frac{L \text{ (in microhenrys)}}{R \text{ (in ohms)}} = t \text{ (in microseconds)}$$

R-C Circuit Time Constant equals

R (ohms) X C (farads) = t (seconds)
R (megohms) x C (microfarads) = t (seconds)
R (ohms) x C (microfarads) = t (microseconds)
R (megohms) x C (micromicrofrads = t (microseconds)

Comparison of Units in Electric and Magnetic Circuits.

	Electric circuit	Magnetic circuit
Force	Volt, E or e.m.f.	Gilberts, F, or m.m.f.
Flow	Ampere, I	Flux, Φ, in maxwells
Opposition	Ohms, R	Reluctance, R
Law	Ohm's law, $I = \frac{E}{R}$	Rowland's law $\Phi = \frac{F}{R}$
Intensity of force	Volts per cm. of length	$H = \frac{1.257IN}{L}$, gilberts per centimeter of length
Density	Current density— for example, amperes per cm^2.	Flux density—for example, lines per cm^2., or gausses

Capacitors in Series
Two capacitors

$$C_T = \frac{C_1 C_2}{C_1 + C_2}$$

More than two

$$\frac{1}{C_T} = \frac{1}{C_1} + \frac{1}{C_2} + \frac{1}{C_3}...$$

Capacitors in Parallel

$$C_T = C_1 + C_2...$$

Capacitive Reactance

$$X_c = \frac{1}{2\pi f C}$$

Impedance in an R-C Circuit (Series)

$$Z = \sqrt{R^2 + X_c^2}$$

Inductors in Series

$$L_T = L_1 + L_2 ... \text{ (No coupling between coils)}$$

Inductors in Parallel
Two inductors

$$L_T = \frac{L_1 L_2}{L_1 + L_2} \text{ (No coupling between coils)}$$

More than two

$$\frac{1}{L_T} = \frac{1}{L_1} + \frac{1}{L_2} + \frac{1}{L_3} ... \text{ (No coupling between coils)}$$

Inductive Reactance

$$X_L = 2\pi f L$$

Q of a Coil

$$Q = \frac{X_L}{R}$$

Impedance of an R-L Circuit (series)

$$Z = \sqrt{R^2 + X_L^2}$$

Impedance with R, C, and L in Series

$$Z = \sqrt{R^2 + (X_L - X_C)^2}$$

Parallel Circuit Impedance

$$Z = \frac{Z_1 Z_2}{Z_1 + Z_2}$$

Sine-Wave Voltage Relationships
Average value

$$E_{ave} = \frac{2}{\pi} \times E_{max} = 0.637 E_{max}$$

91

ELECTRICAL TERMS AND FORMULAS

Effective or r.m.s. value

$$E_{eff} = \frac{E_{max}}{\sqrt{2}} = \frac{E_{max}}{1.414} = 0.707 E_{max} = 1.11 E_{ave}$$

Maximum value

$$E_{max} = \sqrt{2} E_{eff} = 1.414 E_{eff} = 1.57 E_{ave}$$

Voltage in an a-c circuit

$$E = IZ = \frac{P}{I \times P.F.}$$

Current in an a-c circuit

$$I = \frac{E}{Z} = \frac{P}{E \times P.F.}$$

Power in A-C Circuit
Apparent power = EI
True power

$$P = EI \cos \theta = EI \times P.F.$$

Power factor

$$P.F. = \frac{P}{EI} = \cos \theta$$

$$\cos \theta = \frac{\text{true power}}{\text{apparent power}}$$

Transformers
Voltage relationship

$$\frac{E}{E} = \frac{N}{N} \text{ or } E = E \times \frac{N}{N}$$

Current relationship

$$\frac{I_p}{I_s} = \frac{N_s}{N_p}$$

Induced voltage

$$E_{eff} = 4.44 \, BAfN \, 10^{-8}$$

Turns ratio equals

$$\frac{N_p}{N_s} = \sqrt{\frac{Z_p}{Z_s}}$$

Secondary current

$$I_s = I_p \frac{N_p}{N_s}$$

Secondary voltage

$$E_s = E_p \frac{N_s}{N_p}$$

Three Phase Voltage and Current Relationships
With wye connected windings

$$E_{line} = 1.732 E_{coil} = \sqrt{3} E_{coil}$$

$$I_{line} = I_{coil}$$

With delta connected windings

$$E_{line} = E_{coil}$$

$$I_{line} = 1.732 I_{coil}$$

With wye or delta connected winding

$$P_{coil} = E_{coil} I_{coil}$$

$$P_t = 3 P_{coil}$$

$$P_t = 1.732 E_{line} I_{line}$$

(To convert to true power multiply by $\cos \theta$)

Synchronous Speed of Motor

$$\text{r.p.m.} = \frac{120 \times \text{frequency}}{\text{number of poles}}$$

GREEK ALPHABET

Name	Capital	Lower Case	Designates
Alpha	A	α	Angles.
Beta	B	β	Angles, flux density.
Gamma ...	Γ	γ	Conductivity.
Delta	Δ	δ	Variation of a quantity, increment.
Epsilon ...	E	ε	Base of natural logarithms (2.71828).
Zeta	Z	ζ	Impedance, coefficients, coordinates.
Eta	H	η	Hysteresis coefficient, efficiency, magnetizing force.
Theta.....	Θ	θ	Phase angle.
Iota	I	ι	
Kappa	K	κ	Dielectric constant, coupling coefficient, susceptibility.
Lambda ...	Λ	λ	Wavelength.
Mu	M	μ	Permeability, micro, amplification factor.
Nu	N	ν	Reluctivity.
Xi	Ξ	ξ	
Omicron...	O	ο	
Pi	Π	π	3.1416
Rho	P	ρ	Resistivity.
Sigma	Σ	σ	
Tau	T	τ	Time constant, time-phase displacement.
Upsilon ...	Υ	υ	
Phi	Φ	φ	Angles, magnetic flux.
Chi	X	χ	
Psi	Ψ	ψ	Dielectric flux, phase difference.
Omega	Ω	ω	Ohms (capital), angular velocity ($2 \pi f$).

COMMON ABBREVIATIONS AND LETTER SYMBOLS

Term	Abbreviation or Symbol
alternating current (noun)	a.c.
alternating-current (adj.)	a-c
ampere	a.
area	A
audiofrequency (noun)	AF
audiofrequency (adj.)	A-F
capacitance	C
capacitive reactance	X_C
centimeter	cm.
conductance	G
coulomb	Q
counterelectromotive force	c.e.m.f.
current (d-c or r.m.s. value)	I
current (instantaneous value)	i
cycles per second	c.p.s.
dielectric constant	K,k
difference in potential (d-c or r.m.s. value)	E
difference in potential (instantaneous value)	e
direct current (noun)	d.c.
direct-current (adj.)	d-c
electromotive force	e.m.f.
frequency	f
henry	h.
horsepower	hp.
impedance	Z
inductance	L
inductive reactance	X_L
kilovolt	kv.
kilovolt-ampere	kv.-a.
kilowatt	kw.
kilowatt-hour	kw.-hr.
magnetic field intensity	H
magnetomotive force	m.m.f.
megohm	M
microampere	μ a.
microfarad	μ f.
microhenry	μ h.
micromicrofarad	$\mu\mu$ f.
microvolt	μ v.
milliampere	ma.
millihenry	mh.
milliwatt	mw.
mutual inductance	M
power	P
resistance	R
revolutions per minute	r.p.m.
root mean square	r.m.s.
time	t
torque	T
volt	v.
watt	w.

CPSIA information can be obtained
at www.ICGtesting.com
Printed in the USA
LVHW021906171219
640814LV00021B/334